LITTLE FARM IN THE HENHOUSE
A TRUE-LIFE TALE OF HEN-KEEPING ~HOMESTEAD STYLE~

LITTLE FARM IN THE FOOTHILLS
BOOK FOUR

SUSAN COLLEEN BROWNE

WHITETHORN PRESS

Little Farm in the Henhouse: A True-Life Tale of Hen-Keeping ~Homestead Style~

Copyright © 2024 by Susan Colleen Browne

All rights reserved. No part of this book may be used or reproduced in any form without written permission except as brief quotations or excerpts in critical articles and reviews.

Some names of persons appearing in this book have been changed to protect their privacy.

ebook ISBN: 978-1-952470-11-0

Print ISBN (Ingram): 978-1-952470-19-6

Cover Design by Whitethorn Press

Cover photographs © John F. Browne

www.susancolleenbrowne.com

www.susancolleenbrowne.substack.com

ALSO BY SUSAN COLLEEN BROWNE

Village of Ballydara Series

It Only Takes Once

Mother Love

The Hopeful Romantic

The Galway Girls

The Secret Well (A Fairy Cottage Story)

The Christmas Visitor (A Fairy Cottage Story)

The Little Irish Gift Shop

Becoming Emma

Becoming Emma: Special Edition with Two Fairy Cottage Short Stories

The Fairy Cottage of Ballydara

Memoir and Gardening

Little Farm in the Foothills: A Boomer Couple's Search for the Slow Life

Little Farm Homegrown: A Memoir of Food-Growing, Midlife and Self-Reliance on a Small Homestead

Little Farm in the Garden: A Practical Mini-Guide to Raising Selected Fruits and Vegetables Homestead-Style

Middle Grade Fiction

Morgan Carey and The Curse of the Corpse Bride

Morgan Carey and The Mystery of the Christmas Fairies

The Secret Astoria Scavenger Hunt

A NOTE FROM SUSAN

Hello, and welcome to *Little Farm in the Henhouse*, Book 4 of the Little Farm series. It's good to have you here—now we can dish about chickens!

As a former city girl—and a total germaphobe cupcake gardener—I moved out to the Cascade Mountains' Foothills to start a little homestead with my husband John. What little I knew about farm animals was what I'd read in books.

Still, since we were big on self-reliance, deciding to bring chickens to our place seemed like a no-brainer. Yet caring for the three flocks of laying hens we've had over the years has been an absolute eye-opener.

With everything John and I learned, it seemed only right to share those lessons—to help other folks raising a small backyard flock. Although people who simply like chickens might enjoy these stories too!

Yet in the spirit of full disclosure… I wrote about our first flock of hens in *Little Farm Homegrown*, Book 2 of the series. If you've read "Homegrown," Part I of this book might seem familiar to you. And you may be wondering, why revisit our experiences with our first set of chickens?

Well, that's easy to answer. I discovered that each of our flocks—and each individual chicken—has presented different challenges. And teachable moments too. That being the case, I felt strongly that all our chicken experiences belong together.

So instead of picking up where I left off in *Little Farm Homegrown*, with our second flock of pullets, I've included all our stories and lessons—and a few new things—about life with our first hens Dottie, Chloe and Marilyn and the others.

This way, you'll be part of our journey with every one of our girls in one fell swoop... All the struggles and sorrows—yes, there were many—and the joys.

Despite those sorrows, I hope you'll keep reading. Whether you're new to my Little Farm memoirs or my novels, or have already dipped into some of my books, I'm very grateful you've taken a chance with this one.

If you'd like to share your own chicken-keeping wisdom, gardening experiences, or to simply say hi, an easy way is to visit my Little Farm Writer newsletter, www.susancolleenbrowne.substack.com. I would absolutely love to hear from you.

Warm regards and happy hen-keeping!

Susan

INTRODUCING THE LITTLE FARM HENS

*J*ust when you think you know about caring for chickens...

Picture a wooded acreage in a misty valley, surrounded by dark green forested foothills. This woodland property, clearcut twenty or so years ago, is now a riot of alder, maple and evergreens, from saplings to thirty-foot high trees.

Littered with old logging slash and dotted with stumps, the landscape is thickly carpeted with sword fern and Oregon grape. In the summer, tall bracken fern and thimbleberry, and sprawling, thorn-covered blackberry canes makes most of the ten acres nearly impassable.

At least for humans—unless they've come prepared, swathed in thorn-resistant gear and armed with a hatchet, a saw, and a hefty machete!

This woodland acreage, like the surrounding forests, is also teeming with wildlife. You'll find songbirds, deer and rabbits like in any suburban yard. But you'll often see grouse, bald eagles, and red-tailed hawks. And once in a while, bobcats and coyotes, bears and cougars.

In the middle of this ten-acre woodland, up on a ridge, is the little homestead my husband and I call Berryridge Farm. In a fenced clearing, you'll find a modest-sized dark-red rambler and not-quite-matching brick-red, steel-sided shop. Nestled around and between the buildings is my pride and joy: our veggie beds, berry patches, and orchard spaces.

And beyond the garden and orchards, past a cluster of woodsheds, you'll find our chicken compound: a hand-built coop, a caged chicken run, and a roomy fenced yard full of grasses and leafy weeds.

One sunny September afternoon, John and I arrived home in our old Ranger, with five Buff Orpington pullets secured in two boxes. After all the misfortunes with our previous chickens, we were thrilled to have a new set of "girls."

Over the years, our hen-keeping had been a learn-as-you-go kind of experience: caring for our first flock had involved a sharp learning curve, and our second set of hens had been even steeper. But with our five young Buffies, a breed known for their gentle natures, John and I were sure the third time was the charm—that we *finally* knew what we were doing.

Clambering out of the pickup, I couldn't help feeling pleased we had such a nice little home for them. For sure, our coop was nothing fancy—not like the super-cute designer ones you see in magazines, with ingenious little flourishes, entryways and nest boxes.

Although John and I had made a number of improvements to the coop and chicken compound, like an outdoor roost, and a wee, slanted roof over the feeder to keep the girls dry as they ate, our hen digs were simple and utilitarian, like the rest of our place.

That afternoon, John and I gingerly pulled the two boxes out of the truck bed and ferried them into the chicken pen. Indignant thumps and fussing came from the boxes. As we released the five girls, I braced myself for a full-on freakout, like our other hens had done in their new place.

But these chickens didn't seem terribly disturbed, despite the unfamiliar surroundings. As soon as they were on solid ground again, after a bit of hesitation, they started pecking the nearest weeds tentatively, then with a little more gusto. I'd heard Buff Orpingtons were mellower than other chickens, and now, I felt the adaptability of these girls was a good omen!

John and I exchanged grins, then watched the hens, with high hopes they would enjoy their new home. Our new chicken quintet would have larger ranging area than they'd had at our neighbors', who had raised them. And instead of the plain bedding they had before, these hens could scratch in plenty of dirt, greens and other weeds.

Time flew by as we hung out with our girls, and before we knew it, the sun was sinking into the sky. John said, "Well, it's getting late... How about I get dinner started."

"Sounds good," I said. As he strolled back to the house, whistling his usual tune, Beethoven's *Hallelujah Chorus*, I gently herded the birds into their caged area so they could get in a last-minute feed and slurp of water. "Goodnight, girls," I said softly, and closed the door.

With the pen secure, the hens could mosey into their coop for the night whenever they liked.

KNOWING our new girls would be safe, and almost ready to turn in, I quickly tackled the day's postponed garden chores. As usual, I stayed busy until it was too dark to work. Preparing to head into the house, on an impulse, I checked on the hens.

They weren't in the coop!

Panicked, I looked around. Where on earth—

All five were huddled up on the small, slanted roof over the feeder...and not quite asleep, because they kept sliding down!

"Oh, you silly girls!" I said fondly. Almost weak with relief, I knew it was *me* who was silly. I'd assumed the new kids would find their way into the coop…because, well, instinct. Or because the ramp and hen door were pretty much like their previous home.

But clearly, the girls hadn't known there was a coop to sleep in, because I hadn't shown it to them.

Our previous chickens taught me that laying hens like to be up high. Of course they do: they're birds! For example, if you have a roost with two or three levels—like we do—your girls will choose the highest.

At this moment, our new Buffies' adventure up on this three-foot square made perfect sense—when they were ready to go to sleep, they had simply headed for the highest spot they could find.

But of course they couldn't stay there all night.

I opened the coop "people" door, and gently grasped the nearest hen, and removed her from the little roof. One-by-one, I bought them into the coop, and placed each chicken the on the platform beneath their roost. The rest was up to them.

The girls took their time. But eventually figuring out there was indeed a proper roost to sleep on, each hen in turn flapped her wings a bit, jumped up, and clambered onto the roost.

I waited for them to stop flapping and fussing, then ruefully secured the pen. Three flocks in, and we were still learning.

YEARS AGO, when John and I took the giant step forward in "homesteadiness," acquiring what would be our first flock of hens, I wasn't prepared. As I scrambled around a ramshackle little homestead one sunny summer day, to help corral the six hens we'd just purchased, one salient fact slowly dawned on me: chickens were a *lot* of work.

Yet caring for hens, I discovered a new side of myself. It wasn't just city girl me getting a crash-course in chicken-keeping. As the weeks and months unfolded, I took pleasure in caring for them. And I felt new tenderness for the birds that we soon called our "girls."

Later, I realized something else: that if I'd known how ignorant I was about chickens—and wildlife too—I would never have taken the leap!

Despite all my experiences, though, this book isn't an instructional manual—I won't pretend to be an expert with laying hens. Still, I figure I've gained enough know-how that's worth sharing, whether you already have hens, or are thinking of getting a flock.

My own biggest discovery was that you never really stop learning new ways to tend *and* understand your chickens!

In any event, it's my hope that the practical tips and best practices I've picked up along the way will enrich your current or future flock—*and* help make your birds healthy and happy.

But there's something else I want to tell you...

Hen-lovers know that chickens will steal your heart. But too often, as John and I discovered, chickens will break it too. Nature can be cruel, especially when it comes to small-ish, defenseless birds.

So a little word of warning: this book isn't all sweetness and light. In fact, some of the passages may be hard to read.

Yet when it comes to keeping hens, we've found it echoes life generally: Sometimes you have to take the bitter with the sweet.

Now, onward for the tale of the Little Farm hens!

PART I

Six Red Sexlinks

1 * PREDATORS ROAM THE HILLS

Or, Why Chickens Instead of a Dog?

*B*efore we talk about laying hens…
When people learn about our life in the country, one question I get a lot is, "Why don't you have a dog?"

True confession: I've never been much of an animal person.

In my childhood, our family had two dogs. Buddy, an adventurous Springer spaniel who wandered the woodsy neighborhood at will, and a few years later, beagle Snoopy, a cuddly sweetheart. But when I was six years old, before Buddy and Snoopy came along, someone gave us three darling little kittens.

The next-door neighbors had a collie that was once sweet too. Then she came down with distemper. One day, she came into our yard and killed all three kittens. I think that event imprinted in my mind that you couldn't really trust animals.

Still, as a kid, I did love our dogs—although in my free time, when I wasn't playing kickball or climbing trees, I had my head in a book. So I didn't hang out with either pup a whole lot.

Maybe Buddy wasn't too attached to us kids either. He ran off one day, never to be seen again. And Snoopy disappeared from our lives even more suddenly...and tragically. One day, while my siblings and I played in the front yard, Snoopy was goofing around under my mother's car as she prepared to leave on errands. In the midst of the hubbub, she accidentally ran over him.

He died in my younger sister's arms.

My heart ached at losing Snoopy, and in such horrible circumstances. But it wasn't broken in pieces like my sister's was. Yet she didn't let that experience stop her from cherishing many more dogs.

Fast forward to life in the Foothills—a region of three to five thousand-foot thickly forested hills (which in other places might be called "mountains" but here they're called "foothills").

Here, I saw the animal kingdom in a whole new light...and I soon grew attached to the native canines around our place: coyotes. Surrounded as we are by woods, fields, and wetlands, there's plenty of coyote habitat.

As a child, I was raised with the unspoken maxim "children should be seen and not heard." Coyotes, however, live by the opposite—they're frequently *heard* but rarely seen.

The first night John and I spent on our little homestead, coyotes serenaded us for *hours*, with their distinct, shrieky *Yip-Yip-Yah-Yeowww!* In the intervening years, we've often heard coyotes several nights a week, their yipping so deafening it was like they were just outside our windows.

Who knows, maybe they *were* right next to our house. Be that as it may, their racket, as I've observed before, is like how a dog might sound giving birth upside down.

I've since learned some interesting coyote factoids. While coyotes are closely related to dogs, unlike domesticated dogs, they form little family units. Coyotes mate for life, and both parents stick around to raise the pups—even the older siblings help out! But also *unlike* dogs, coyotes are extremely canny about keeping out of sight. So despite all their attention-getting hullabaloo, I've rarely seen them near our place.

On my daily bikerides, though, past dense forests and a large wild meadow, I'll catch sight of a coyote every couple of months, their pert little faces every bit as engaging as a dog's. What's even more fascinating to me, given their little families, is that I've never, *ever* seen their young. Or more than one coyote at a time.

Cycling a couple of years back, I encountered one right in the middle of the main road. I slowed down, to give the animal a chance to melt into the underbrush as the coyotes I've spotted usually do. Instead, the coyote gave me a long look, then simply carried on, trotting ahead of me in the center of the pavement.

How curious! Luckily, there was no traffic. I gave the coyote lots of space, and followed slowly, keeping a close eye on it. I really wanted to see just how far the critter would meander up the middle of the road.

Quite a ways, as it turned out. As the minutes ticked by, the coyote briskly trotted along, glancing over its shoulder at me every so often. It did this for another half mile! Then finally it gave me one last look, and wandered into the brush.

This experience had me smiling *and* shaking my head the rest of the day.

Still, long story short: although I'm very fond of the wildlife here, like I said, I've never really been an animal person. Babies have always been my thing.

Starting at age seven, when I wasn't at school I was babysitting my toddler brother. When my baby sister came along a few years later, I became a quasi-parent to her as well. At twenty-two, I became a mother for real, and by my mid-forties, I was a grandmother. So kiddos, not critters, have always been on my radar.

And to be even more truthful, as time went by I enjoyed

dogs in general less and less. You see, I've been a lifelong, almost daily bikerider. And anyone who cycles knows that you are often a dog-magnet. Unfortunately, it's not friendly dogs that chase people; it's the aggressive ones.

And yours truly has been chased, menaced, and even bitten by more mean dogs than I care to count.

(A side note: you may be wondering, if I encounter problem mutts, why don't I just take another route? In our neighborhood, the gigantic foothills mean our main road only goes in two directions. No side roads, no alternate routes, no shortcuts.)

Anyway. Despite my history, with our new life in the boondocks, I soon grew fond of the neighborhood domestic dogs. Fiona, a super-friendly golden retriever, gave me new faith in canine companions. Our closest neighbor's pup, a blue heeler named Nellie, became John's pal.

He'd be clearing brush in the woods, and over she'd come with a stick in her mouth. He'd throw the stick, Nellie would fetch it, and of course, being a breed who likes having a job, she wanted to do it All. Day. Long.

I'm well aware too, that being a dog owner, a good, loving one, is a big commitment. It's not like back in the day when you'd get a neighbor's extra puppy or bring a dog home from the pound. You didn't bother much with veterinary care, spaying or proper training, or the other doggie necessaries for fully enjoying your pet.

As more grandchildren came along, and I took on more grandmotherly responsibilities, the idea of getting a dog seemed more and more overwhelming. I already felt time-challenged with my writing business and looking after our place—how would I fit in all the new obligations of having a pet?

Even if a dog could help chase rabbits and rodents away from our garden, our little homestead needed my time and energy more than we needed a dog.

There was one more inescapable aspect of our life here. The

longer we lived in the Foothills, the more horror stories we heard about dogs and predators.

I have a friend who also lives in the Foothills, about eight miles away. Her home is in a one-acre clearing surrounded by six acres of tall, old firs. She has a lovely dog Dipper, an energetic border collie mix. Dipper isn't the size of an Irish Wolfhound or anything, but she's no teacup Yorkie either.

One day, my friend caught a mountain lion right in the middle of their yard, creeping up on Dipper. It was a close call, but her quick intervention got Dipper safely into the house.

Other dogs we knew weren't as lucky. Nellie the neighbor dog got a new doggie sibling—Ernie, a sturdy Shar Pei bigger than Dipper. Despite our neighbor's precautions, one day a mountain lion attacked Ernie from behind. Our neighbor rushed him to the vet, but he nearly didn't make it.

Although he survived the attack, he was never the same.

Our farmer neighbors down the hill had a feisty little Chihuahua. They kept a close eye on her, but one day, right in their backyard a red-tailed hawk dove for her. They chased it off just in time. Another day, though, the little dog wasn't so lucky. She got out again and a bobcat nabbed her. Sadly, she was killed instantly.

As for keeping a dog to chase off wildlife—well, it doesn't always work. For years, another neighbor had a dozen chickens in a seemingly secure little compound. Their border collie was a reliable watchdog, guarding their place every waking moment. Yet bobcats still managed to carry off their hens one by one.

Now, I know coyotes will go after small animals too. So whether it's coyotes or the other big cat predators in our neighborhood, who's to say any dog of ours that we loved and cared for, would not eventually become wild critter chow?

Even with the risks, though, and all our outside family commitments, in our early Foothill years, John and I would talk about getting a dog. But life has continued to grow more complicated; helping with aging relatives and grandchildren means more time away from our place, not less. And John and I knew leaving a dog home alone too much was a recipe for a bored, unhappy pet.

Then, about four years into our homesteady life, the idea of a dog pretty much faded away. In its place, John and I toyed with the idea of a new phase for our place: getting laying hens! Chickens would be less work than a dog, I was sure.

And with my Pollyanna tendency toward wild-eyed optimism—since I had no idea how to look after hens—I thought, why not?

2 * GETTING CHICKENS: ONE STEP AT A TIME

*N*aturally, John and I liked farm animals...in *theory*. Being city people, however, we knew little about taking care of them. We definitely needed to *learn* about chickens before acting on our big plan.

STEP 1: Education

One hot morning in August, we piled into the Ranger and drove across the county to the regional agricultural fair. Always keen to get a closer look at farm critters, we headed straight for the chicken house.

I'll admit, seeing chickens looking their best, poking around their super-tidy cages, hovered over by clean-cut, 4-H teens, might have given me a pretty idealized view of what keeping hens was all about. Still, the fair was a helpful starting point.

Two months later, after finishing our fall garden chores, being book people, John and I embraced the next phase: *reading about chickens.*

We spent the winter deep-diving into backyard farming books. Our top picks, *Animal Vegetable Miracle* by Barbara Kingsolver, and *Farm City* by Novella Carpenter, were a revelation. While both focused on small-scale poultry-raising, Kingsolver kept hens and turkeys at her idyllic Virginia homestead, in a lovely hollow in the Appalachian mountains.

Carpenter's experience was as different as night and day: urban farming in the center of Oakland, California. She raised her chicken and turkey chicks in her bathtub and kept them on the deck of her apartment.

Carpenter had a couple of pigs too, which I learned require *ginormous* amounts of food. Apparently she obtained her pig feed by dumpster-diving behind restaurants.

The most hilarious chapter was the time she took a baby turkey on an airline flight, and hid it in her shirt! Needless to say, she walked around all that day with turkey poo on her front.

While I didn't feel confident enough to get a large flock like Kingsolver, and would most certainly never, *ever* follow in Carpenter's footsteps with house poultry, surely there was no reason John and I couldn't keep a few hens in our little corner of paradise!

We were eager for this new facet of self-sufficiency—after all, we were big egg eaters, John especially. Having one less item to buy at the grocery store was the frosting on the cake.

Six chickens sounded about right—I was *sure* so few would be very little trouble. Country life had tamed the worst of my germ fears, so I felt primed to deal with a bit of animal manure.

And on the off-chance of a zombie apocalypse coming along (or any other kind of breakdown of modern life as we know it), John, I, and our family, could hunker down on our place and still survive! At any rate, with on-site egg producers, we would have some good quality protein to sustain us.

By early spring, John and I made a final, no-backsies commitment to getting hens. Immediately, he began tinkerdoodling with ideas for a chicken coop.

Luckily, we'd saved our income tax return to pay for our project. Not that it was a lot of money; we had to quickly nix a pre-made chicken house. Besides, for John, no catalogue-kit would do. By the spring thaw, he came up with a final coop design.

Step 2: Building the Coop

John had already completed several three-sided woodsheds, but the henhouse would be his first fully-enclosed structure. At 8' by 8', it would be the largest building you can construct in our county without needing a permit. Half the building would be the chickens' living area, and the other half for garden equipment and chicken supplies. Really, a homestead can never have enough storage!

For the walls, John used siding panels made of pressboard coated with primer on one side. He cut out three good-sized windows for the whole structure. The two windows in the coop, he covered with poultry fencing for safety, and made one-piece shutters for each one with more siding material, hinged at the top.

For the third window, in the storage half, John installed a sheet of Plexiglass, then built a partition between the coop and the storage area: a wall for the lower portion, but he kept the upper third open, and covered that with poultry wire as well.

With windows on all four sides, the hens would have plenty of ventilation. And with those openings covered with fencing, the coop would be safe as houses.

Since John and I decided *not* to build this project on the cheap, he installed a steel roof for the coop, giving it a decent pitch so rain and snow would slide off.

The final touch was distributing a layer of crushed rock

along the interior walls, providing drainage for the dirt floor. *And* hopefully prevent small critters from trying to dig inside.

Once finished, John's hand-built chicken coop was even sturdier than his woodsheds—it reminded me of one of those slightly battered, 50s-era Chevy trucks that aren't pretty, but last forever.

Now that the coop was complete, he started on what we called the "safety zone," an 8' by 18' caged run leading from the coop, where we would keep our birds' feeder and waterer. John enclosed the run on all four sides with poultry wire and steer fencing; it was topped by steer fencing as well.

To keep the chicken feed dry, he fashioned a little three-foot square roof over the feeder (that I mentioned previously), attaching it just under the Plexiglass window. On the underside, he added a hook to hang the feeder on. The hens would be comfortable while they ate too!

Adjacent to the run, he created another uncovered "chicken exercise yard," with a doorway leading to our newest orchard space. Our future chickens would have lots of room to explore outside their compound.

To give the whole area a finished look, John lined the perimeter of the chicken yard with more crushed rock. As he spread out his final wheelbarrow load, I met him at the fence, grinning ear-to-ear. "It looks amazing—so neat and tidy!"

He tried to look modest, but I could tell he was really pleased with the result. "Not bad, huh?"

Last came the coop's interior "amenities." John constructed a roost, attaching three dowels to a three-foot high frame in a stair-step arrangement, which took up most of the coop's space. He cut an opening for what's called a man door (I prefer "people door") leading into the safety zone. Using a piece of siding for the door, he added hinges on one side.

Since hens like their own chicken-sized entry and exit, John carved out another small opening about a foot and a half off the ground. An extra piece of siding served as a ramp up to the hen door.

Meanwhile, I'd been studying up on all kinds of chicken husbandry, and showed John photos of nesting structures. "This one looks doable," I said, pointing to one design: nest boxes on the outside of the coop. Although I'd grown more comfortable around animals, I was secretly relieved I wouldn't have to go *inside* the coop every day.

John built an oblong box big enough for three nests and attached it to the north side of the coop, about three and a half feet off the ground, then added a little hinged top. A hen would have all the privacy she needed to lay.

Now what we needed were some actual *chickens*.

Step 3: Hen Shopping

After John completed what I thought was a genius chicken compound, I could see he was far more into our chicken project than I'd ever hoped. To surprise him, on the down-low I'd been making some phone calls. I got the name of a gal who supervised the youth livestock program at the county fair and asked her about buying grown chickens.

To my delight, she gave me the number of a local chicken farmer. When I called the farmer, she said she wasn't selling any hens, but she had a friend, Shannon, with a flock in the Foothills south of us, and gave me her email.

After our initial flurry of messages, I connected with Shannon by phone. I discovered she was Scottish, and was every bit as nice as she seemed in her emails.

She and her family lived on a homestead about twenty-five miles away, and she would have some pullets ready by early summer. I told her we were hoping for six chickens, and asked how much she wanted for them.

"What do you think of fifteen dollars each?" she said.

I'd learned pullets are young hens that are just starting to lay, and that their eggs can be more nutritious than mature hens'. For sure, $15.00 per bird was a steal! "Sounds great," I told her. "When will they be ready?"

"Not until July," she said regretfully. "I know that's a long time to wait—why don't you come out and see them?"

After settling on a date, I thanked her and hung up, almost rubbing my hands in anticipation. As someone who hates shopping, I've never been good with gift giving. But John's birthday was approaching, and after all these years, I could finally give him something special—which would require no shopping whatsoever!

3 * A BIRTHDAY GIFT LIKE NO OTHER

The afternoon of John's birthday, one warm June day, I asked him ever-so-casually, "How about a nice country drive before dinner?"

My easygoing husband said "yes" right away. He guessed something was up, but was nice enough not to spoil any surprise I might have in mind. We climbed into his '97 Ford Ranger and headed for the river valley south of us.

Verdant farmlands stretched on either side of the two-lane highway, while to the east, billowing clouds gathered above the dark green foothills. Following Shannon's directions, we turned off the main road, traversed another narrow, low-lying road that was still covered with water from the spring rains. Turning right, we pootled along a curvy lane tucked against a wooded hill. After another mile or two, I saw a mailbox with Shannon's house number. "This is it!"

We bounced into Shannon's driveway and gazed around. Her place seemed like a much *realer* homestead than ours, with a picturesque, one-story wood cabin, and a higgledy-piggledy assortment of pens and farm animals and roaming dogs.

The homestead was dominated by a large chicken run. Bare

of vegetation, the pen was filled with strawberry-blond chickens. A coop four times the size John had built stood in the center, the whole area covered with heavy black commercial fishing net—the kind Alaskan fisher-people use to catch fifty-pound halibut!

Clearly, this part of the Foothills was home to the same raptors and predators we had in our neighborhood. Outside the run, near the hillside, was a plot of thigh-high grass.

On the near side of the chicken pen, a few sheep grazed in another fenced area, and a small hillock surrounded with a split-rail fence held four or five goats, one standing atop a pile of dirt. As John and I climbed out of the truck, a lanky Vizsla, a smaller mixed-breed, and a terrier ran over to us, all barking vociferously.

Shannon stepped out of the house to greet us, shushing the dogs. A pretty, thirty-something woman with short brown hair, Shannon had two young boys at her side, who were about four and six years old. After we introduced ourselves, she showed us around, her youngest son trailing us, the Vizsla galloping all over the place.

Together, we ambled to the makeshift fence around the goats, Shannon joking that since there's never been a fence invented that will hold goats, why try? She waved toward the Vizsla, who seemed to be everywhere at once. "He's a great watchdog—nothing gets close to our animals anyway."

The goats probably roamed all over the place too; I saw animal droppings wherever I looked. Glad I'd worn my oldest pair of gardening boots, we entered the chicken run to get a closer view of her operation.

Fifty or so clucking chickens busily pecked the ground. Feeling anxious surrounded by So. Many. Birds, I watched nervously as some pecked each other. I tried to keep my distance as others flapped their wings or skittered around. "All of them are Sexlinks," said Shannon.

She went on to explain that despite the strange name, they're a breed known for good egg production. The birds were certainly attractive, their feathers a hundred shades of red-blond. I carefully picked my way to the coop for a peek inside, and Shannon showed us her nest boxes. I did wonder why the nests were at the ground level—easier to build, maybe?—but didn't say anything.

She took us over to a barbed wire pen a short walk from the chicken run, where two porkies wallowed in the mud. Stepping inside, Shannon scratched them between the ears, wearing a fond smile. "Pigs are a lot of fun—really intelligent."

John drew closer. "I see you've got a solar panel here."

The panel was about the size of a magazine. "Yes," Shannon replied, "it's to power the fence, to keep the pigs in."

Very smart, I thought, not having to run an electric line down the middle of your homestead—although these two peaceable-looking critters didn't look like they were eager to escape.

On the way back to the house, her little boy approached us. "Look what I found, Mommy." He held a dead chicken in his arms.

"Go get rid of that!" Shannon scolded. She waved toward a brushy area on the other side of the house. "And wash your hands!" she called as he ran off. "Sorry about that," she said to us, looking nonplussed but not terribly worried. "I'll take a look at the hen later," she added, then the phone rang inside the cabin. "Can you give me a minute?"

"Sure," John and I said at the same time. With our hostess away, I glanced back at the run. All of the birds appeared vigorous and healthy, despite what seemed like a dog-eat-dog existence. The dead bird had showed no sign of injury.

And since Shannon had been so highly recommended by the chicken farmer, it seemed really unlikely that she'd sell us sick birds. Maybe, I thought, chickens were like a lot of other animals. Sometimes you ended up with a few runts or weaklings that just couldn't make it.

With Shannon still in the house, I checked out her vegetable patch, close to the road. Covered with bird netting draped on poles, the garden was like the homestead itself, somewhat messy but the kale looked healthy, and you could see small squashes here and there.

Off to one side was a much smaller, wire-enclosed pen, holding a couple of dozen all-white chickens.

From my research, I knew they were meat birds. But now, I could see how different they were from layers. Huddled in a mass in the far corner of the pen, the chickens trembled like a vibrating feather pillow. The red-blond hens seemed like scrappy critters, but this bunch seemed like they'd have trouble surviving an itty-bitty rainstorm.

By the time Shannon emerged, I had fetched our checkbook from the truck so we could pay her in advance. Thanking us, she said, "The chickens should start to lay in another month—let's touch base then."

We shook on the deal, and John and I climbed back into the Ranger. Despite desperately wanting to wash my hands, I was so excited about our future chickens I *almost* forgot my germiphobiness.

ON THE WAY home John pulled up at our locally-owned farmer supply store. We had chicken equipment to buy! And I quickly decided I could actually enjoy shopping after all, if I it was at a store for farmers.

After stepping carefully around Shannon's chicken pen, dotted with bird droppings, I had one big priority: muck boots for both of us—our first real farmer's footgear. Next, into our oversized shopping cart went a chicken feeder and a waterer, both of galvanized steel, along with a bag of grit for the hens' digestion and oyster shell flakes to make strong eggshells.

Finally, we drove around to the back of the store to pick up a fifty-pound sack of feed pellets and a bale of straw for bedding. Our grand total came to $234—the last of our tax return.

But what did we care? We were ready for our chicken adventure!

4 * GETTING TO KNOW OUR HENS

Five weeks later, on a sunny Saturday, John and I headed south again. In the bed of the Ranger sat three durable, nearly pristine boxes we'd saved from our house move years before. When we pulled up at Shannon's place for the second time, she was ready for us.

The chickens, however, were not. The pullets she'd chosen for us were stubbornly resistant to being apprehended. A couple of them scrambled into the tall grass.

"Hiding spots from the hawks," Shannon told us, as her older boy ran after the birds. John and I brought our boxes over to the run, then watched the two skilled chicken-chasers.

Rounding up the escapees took about twenty minutes, but finally, Shannon and her son had captured six chickens. As the birds flapped their wings and *buck-bucked* raucously, Shannon, with John's help, got two birds in each box.

Taping up the tops, John left several inches open between the cardboard slats for air. He and I loaded the boxes into the truck bed, and said our farewells to Shannon and her son.

When we arrived back at our place, the hens were banging around inside their containers. Once we carried the boxes to the chicken compound, John opened them, the birds squawking and flapping their wings the whole time, pecking him as he released them into their new run. I cringed to see the previously clean cardboard soiled with manure. I mean, the drive had only been forty-five minutes! Couldn't they hold it that long?

Watching our new flock, feeling somewhere between charmed and apprehensive, I reminded myself that ruined cardboard was a tiny price to pay for farm-fresh, homegrown eggs. Our hens didn't know it yet, but they were going to be treated to a great life. Even if their new place was homemade and looked it, the chickens would reside in what I liked to think was a veritable luxury chicken resort.

LEARNING a Hen-Keeping Routine

I can't *believe* I once thought a dog would be more work than chickens.

I soon discovered keeping a small flock of hens was a *far* bigger deal than I had ever guessed. The first week or two, I had to get used to simply being around chickens. Stepping into their pen, I would feel intimidated—and frankly annoyed when the girls pecked at my hands and legs.

Later, I learned that hens explore their world through their beaks. Pecking around at everything within reach—including you—doesn't mean they're being aggressive. Chickens are simply trying to figure out what they're dealing with, whether it's a new or different human, food, or environment.

John, being of sterner stuff, didn't mind a few pecks. He would often sit on a stump in our newest orchard where we let the chickens scratch all day, and take a bird up on his knee. In fact, he sort of doted on them—and he was always looking at ways he could improve the compound.

In the coop, he noticed the birds struggling a bit to jump

from the floor to the roost. So John added a little platform just inside the hen door: an 18" x 18" piece of siding.

He also made some tweaks to the compound's two people doors—one that led into the caged run, and the one leading into the coop: he adjusted the hinges so the doors would swing more freely, and made the latches more secure.

Despite my inexperience with animals, it actually wasn't long before I clicked with our birds. Since they'd become a big part of our lives, of course we had to give them names.

John called the biggest, most assertive hen Chloe O'Brien, after a character on his latest favorite TV show, "24." (The human Chloe O'B. could kick butt too.) The lightest-blond one was Marilyn (as in Monroe), and two we couldn't tell apart were Daisy and Maisy.

Girl #5 was a dark honey color with one small white dot on her thigh, so she became Dottie. Then we seemed to run out of inspiration, and never did come up with a name for the last one.

Yet there were several elements to keeping hens that I hadn't anticipated.

FIRST, was that they poo *constantly*. Not to be too graphic, but they drop something every few minutes, and *everywhere*. Big piles, small ones, and everything in between.

I wasn't prepared for the extra noise they brought to our place either. You see, silence was my *jam*. The quieter the better. You couldn't consider the birdsong filling the air of Berryridge Farm *noise*—like the wind in the trees, wild birds created the symphony of the woods.

The hens? Not so much. The steady clucking, their *buck-buck-buck-buh-GAH*, the startling *Squawk!* when a bird got pecked by her sister, and the constant squeaking of the feeder broke into my peace. Yet all the sounds soon became part of the background music of our place.

The biggest surprise, though, was a positive one: the hens were great company! I liked watching their endearing little waddle-stride, and when you entered the pen, they'd come running like they adored the ground you walked on, jockeying for who could get the closest to the door before you opened it.

Of course, I knew it was because their "human" was bringing them food, but still.

They were entertaining too. Hens, I soon discovered, are inquisitive creatures, and our girls didn't waste time exploring their world. They were particularly drawn to the slanted little roof over the feeder—which as I mentioned before, John added to keep them dry while they ate. Made of primer-coated pressboard, the surface of the overhang was really slippery. But there was a Plexiglass window right next to the top, looking into the storage shed adjoining the coop.

Apparently our chickens found the window interesting enough to risk the uncertain footing. Many times, I watched with amusement as a hen or two would climb up on the overhang, only to invariably slip, claws scritching on the pressboard. Still, the hen would gamely scramble back up the little roof, clearly determined to stay at the top.

Could they see their reflections in the window, I wondered? Maybe they were curious about what the heck that "other bird" was doing!

Most rewarding of all was how the girls would follow you around loyally, making you feel even more wanted and needed —although the way they got underfoot was not only awkward, but often hazardous! And just as our chicken lady Shannon had predicted, the girls started laying soon after we got them home.

Problem: they were laying everywhere but in their nest boxes! If there were any secluded spots inside the coop or behind the old stump in the run, the girls would settle in and deposit their eggs there.

However, with a bit of research we found an easy solution: you simply set a decoy "egg" in the nests.

Who knew? I scrabbled around in my holiday supplies and found a beige plastic Easter egg, the kind you can take apart to put candy in. I placed the empty egg in one of the nest boxes, and what do you know: within a couple of days the girls realized the nest was where they were *supposed* to lay!

Their eggs were large brown beauties, the yolks a rich yellow-orange, and each day brought at least three or four freshly laid ones. All in all, John and I felt we'd made a quantum leap in the homesteading biz.

5 * CHICKEN COSTS: MONEY, TIME AND ENERGY

*L*ike I said before, our six birds were *work*. Fresh feed every day, and refreshing their water supply every couple of days. The waterer needed cleaning and sanitizing at least once a week, and more often in hot weather.

On rainy days, I didn't always feel like putting on my work pants and muck boots to go into their pen, but there the girls were—letting you know, quite vocally, that they didn't like being neglected.

We soon found out they didn't like getting wet either. John and I draped a tarp over about half of the steer wire roof of the safety zone, which would keep half the area nice and dry.

The hens were *messy*. Although I learned scratching is a healthy chicken behavior, it was disconcerting to see how compulsively chickens tear up the ground. During our flock's first night in the coop, they obliterated the tidy row of gravel John had arranged so carefully, rocks scattered all over the dirt floor. Within a couple of days, ditto for the gravel John had laid so neatly around their pen.

Most eye-opening of all: chickens weren't a cheap date.

John and I had purchased only the one sack of feed pellets. When it was nearly empty, I examined the feed more closely, and didn't much care for the way it looked—the pellets didn't seem to contain any recognizable food particles. Time to read the label: the ingredients were mostly processed corn and soy, with vitamins and other chemically-sounding stuff.

I decided then and there that if you're going organic with your homestead, you might as well go all the way.

Connecting with a bunch of local chicken people by email, I found certified organic feed from a new, boutique feed business in the city an hour's drive away. The layer mix was chock-full of raw, unprocessed grains you *could* identify, split green and yellow peas, oyster shell bits for calcium, and what I guessed to be a protein/vitamin meal.

This organic preparation was packaged in an environmentally-friendly brown bag made of several layers of paper.

I was more than pleased with the quality—yet I hadn't quite been prepared for the price. The fifty pound sack of pellets from the farm store had cost about the same as a big hamburger and fries at a fast-food restaurant. Let's say, "$."

The cost for the organic stuff was, *gulp*, more like a dinner at a fine dining establishment! Say, closer to "$$$." Plus you only got twenty-five pounds, even if it was soy-free. A same-size sack of organic chicken scratch—that's just raw grains—was more like "$$."

This particular feed wasn't easy to obtain either. Since it was unavailable in retail, the chicken people I mentioned had formed a buying co-op, and invited John and me to join. Which was great, even if it was a bit of a hassle. When it was time to replenish our supply, first we had to connect with the co-op's coordinator, then time our pick-up with *her* schedule *and* our trips to town.

A few months later, the business started selling their feed at their warehouse. So now, instead of a two-hour round trip to pick up an order at someone's house, John and I found ourselves with the same time suck, to get it wholesale.

We *probably* could have found something less expensive, maybe not totally organic, maybe not soy-free. Still, being committed to supporting local products, we stuck with this brand.

Yet the real challenge with chickens wasn't the cost of their feed, or the time spent buying supplies. Or even tending them daily.

It was cleaning the coop.

THE JOB FELL to me by default: between John and me, I was the one small enough to squeeze inside the coop and work around the large, three-rung roost. So despite my dread of germs, every other day, rain or shine, I would don my coop clothes.

Besides my stained Carhartt pants, I wore a hoodie over my tee-shirt with the hood securely pulled up, with another long-sleeved fleece on top of it. I put a broad-brimmed hat on top of my hood, then elbow-high rubber gloves. I wore this get-up even on the hottest days, you understand. Although my pathogen-avoidance had improved, I never claimed to be cured, did I?

Carefully maneuvering around the roost, peering in every corner, I found there was guano not only *on* the roost, but splashed on every wall. (I never did figure out how the chickens managed that. And they weren't telling. Obviously what happens in the coop stays in the coop.)

For poo-scooping, I appropriated a garden tool from our collection, a beautifully made curved trowel with a varnished wooden handle from Williams-Sonoma—a gift from John's daughter. I just hoped she would never find out what we used it for.

Despite the window openings, the coop was dim inside. I'd

pick up the most obvious piles of manure off the dirt floor to dump into a pail, then squint at the gravel the hens had scattered all over the place, trying to figure out what was a rock and what was poo.

"There's got to be a better way," I said to John one night, and showed him another roost design. He liked it, but the coop was pretty much a done deal. See, for any new manure-catching system, he'd have to disassemble the roost, but he couldn't really fit inside the coop to do it!

We also discovered our biggest design error—the nesting boxes—and why Shannon's boxes had been at ground level.

I already talked about how hens prefer to be up high. A laying hen likes to be the top dog, and a flock has a definite pecking order—it's not a play on words, but a real fact.

When it's time for the hens to go to sleep, the highest perch on the roost is the most desirable spot, taken by the leaders of the flock. The less assertive birds are then forced to roost on the lower rungs.

Turns out, the top of our roost held four birds, maybe five if they cozied up. So any bird slow to turn in at dusk would be stuck on the second rung.

It was usually Dottie, the most sociable but most submissive of our flock. She'd hang around with John and me well into the evening, often until it was nearly dark, the time we went inside. We soon discovered that she'd figured out a way to score a top spot after all—having a lovely repose exactly where she wasn't supposed to: in one of the nesting boxes.

But what did she know? It was at about the same height as the roost, so naturally she figured it was for sleeping. Now we had to figure out how to train her to sleep on the roost.

AFTER LEARNING that our nesting boxes should have been placed considerably lower than the roost, John and I discovered something else about their sleeping habits. As if it wasn't bad enough that chickens poo all over the place, we found out they do most of it while they sleep!

Naturally, if Dottie or any other girl was sleeping in a box, any egg laid the next morning would be right in the mess the guilty parties had deposited in the night. Clearly, the nest boxes needed a re-do, but in the middle of all our late summer chores, John and I didn't have time to tear up the coop for the job.

We checked our chicken-raising books and found a way around the problem: a nest guard. John created a moveable mini-fence with a rope attached to it. From outside the coop, you could pull on the rope to raise and lower the guard as needed.

It wasn't convenient; you'd have to make sure the guard was secured before the chickens retired for the evening. Then, to give them access to the nests by early morning, you'd have to go back outside at night, to lower the guard after they fell asleep.

But John's design seemed to do the trick. That is, unless a bird roused in the night and snuck back into a nest. After he placed a piece of siding to slide under the top roost to catch some of the nightly manure, the coop was much easier to clean. I was able to dial down my cleaning to twice a week, giving me more time for other chores.

With all the chicken-keeping research and reading I was doing, I realized the poultry-raising author Novella Carpenter (the one who carried a baby turkey inside her shirt), wasn't unique. Lots of hen lovers frequently cuddled their chickens and carried them around. Not only that, but some true hen fanciers brought their birds into their home!

Since hens poo every other minute, and as far as I knew could not, and more importantly *would* not wear little diapers (not like a pet monkey), I just didn't *get* how people could live with bird droppings all over their house.

I was fond of our little girls, but to John and me, they were farm animals. Not pets. Despite our mistakes, though, a few months into our hen-keeping, John and I felt we had this chicken thing down pat.

But with fall came a fresh learning curve.

6 * STEPPING UP OUR CHICKEN GAME

*A*s the fall rains began, John and I had a major scare: we found scads of feathers all over the coop and compound! The girls looked scraggly and unwell; some even had bare patches of skin showing.

Was something wrong with them? And if they *weren't* sick, and dropping feathers was completely normal, why on earth would hens lose their insulation with winter coming?

We soon learned this loss of feathers is called "molting"—part of a laying hen's natural cycle. That's when a hen's feathers gradually fall out, and a new set grows in. At the same time, as the days grow shorter and colder, egg production drops.

I didn't mind fewer eggs for a while; John and I could finally use up the stash we'd built up since the summer. And this molting thing was apparently part of the changing seasons, all good. But it soon dawned on me that I missed warm weather like I never had before.

Because summer hen-keeping was world's away from cold weather care.

As the sodden days followed one after another, the hens'

digs, which at the outset we thought were the cat's meow, actually needed adjusting yet *again*.

The most pressing problem was our outside access to the nests. It was right under the coop's overhanging roof, and as a result, collecting eggs in wet weather meant getting absolutely *drenched*. This tweak was really a *well, duh*, and John promptly installed a gutter along the roofline, right above the nest boxes.

As it often happens, though—you solve one problem and another appears.

REMEMBER the tarp John and I draped over the hens' run? We soon found it didn't keep the hens dry like we'd planned. Since the plastic wasn't perfectly taut, when it rained—which is almost daily during our winters—John or I would have to change into outdoor gear, trudge through the rain and mud, and push up on the tarp where puddles had formed. Despite doing this tarp management several times a day, the puddles soon led to leaks.

The hens seemed to do all right during cold-ish dry spells, but when another January Northeaster dropped the temperatures into the teens, John and I felt downright guilty about their unheated coop. He rigged up a rudimentary heater he'd seen his dad create: a 60-watt incandescent bulb set inside a coffee can, with holes punched in the can to let heat escape.

After John connected his makeshift heater to a 200-foot industrial-strength extension cord, he plugged it into one of the shop's outlets. And what do you know, that bit of heat seemed to liven up the flock.

Not that a little warmth had any effect on the piles of manure in the coop. When temperatures dropped to the 20s or below, coop cleaning, never a fun chore, became even more unpleasant: the girls' poo just froze solid.

However, that fancy Williams-Sonoma trowel with the

pointy end really came in handy. Instead of trying to scrape frozen manure off the coop board (which never worked), with a little elbow grease, you could chip the poo loose.

I had to change out my rubber gloves for insulated winter work gloves, but nothing would keep my hands warm. By the time I'd finished the coop cleaning, my fingers would be like Popsicles.

Ever mindful of the girls' comfort in cold weather, John and I noticed that as much as our hens disliked getting wet, there was something they hated more: Snow.

Interestingly, in dry weather, they would spend even the coldest days outdoors. When it came to snow, though, all six of them would not so much as step foot—or claw—into it. I wondered if it's because their feet are composed of only cartilage, without flesh or fat for insulation.

But the fact remained: when it snowed they would simply mill around in the small, un-snowy spots under the leaky tarp.

And the limited areas weren't enough. When wind blew the snow inside the pen, the girls would congregate under the little roof above the feeder, which meant the chicken-poo patties were much more concentrated. Surely this mix of mud and manure in the run, so unpleasant to walk in, couldn't possibly be a healthy environment for hens.

In the Foothills, when we get snow, it generally starts to melt within a week. A heavy snowfall would make the tarp even *more* saggy, and as the snow turned to water, well—there we were, dealing with more leaks and mud.

John devised a solution for both the hens' health *and* their snow aversion: he created a miniature outdoor roost. He set a horizontal trowel on a sturdy structure about two feet off the ground, and covered it with a wee pitched roof.

They could keep their feet dry when it rained, and even on the snowiest days they could hang out in the run without getting cold feet.

Once the little roost was finished, of course I had to go out and admire John's handiwork. "It's really cute!"

He grinned. "Well, if we didn't feel like homesteaders before, we sure do now that we have animals."

WITH THE ONSET OF SPRING, the hens were happily settling back into scratching up every shred of vegetation in their pen. Luckily, our newest orchard space, adjacent to it, was a perfect roaming spot for our girls. In the bare spots they created, they would dig little depressions in the dirt for dust baths.

Dust baths are an instinctive habit. Hens will scratch up a hole big enough to settle into, then flap their wings and sort of squeegee down into the dirt. The soil will then shift in between their feathers and even reach their skin. Apparently this action helps eliminate pests and parasites from the neck down.

To create more areas for dust baths, John built a narrow, fenced-in "tunnel" adjacent to our woodshed complex. Now the hens had even more safe *and* dry spots. The girls also liked to hang out beneath a young, yet robust fir tree that stood at the edge of the orchard—another secure, dry spot for dust-bathing.

Luckily, with all this soil-scrabbling, the birds didn't bother our orchard trees. Besides, a little chicken manure here and there would surely invigorate the trees' growth. While the hens were able to fly very short distances, they didn't seem interested in breaching the four-foot fence separating the orchard from our main garden.

In their own ranging areas, the girls went gaga over the first spring weeds, dandelions and wild spinach—and provided a couple of new benefits John and I didn't predict. First, the weeds didn't get a chance to go to seed and spread into our food garden. After a few weeks of constant scratching, though, they'd devoured every shred of green.

And along came the second benefit: weeding our veggie beds

changed from a chore into a fun way to forage for hen food! John and I would bring the girls handfuls of greens and they'd happily fight over them.

They loved bugs and worms of every kind too. I'm sure they scarfed down some beneficial bugs, but I'm also positive they eliminated lots of insect pests too. In any case, beware the poor beetle who ventured into their lair!

Between their feed, the scratch grains, *and* the weeds and bugs, they ate pretty much constantly. With all this nice organic fuel, they were back to laying like crazy, at least four or five eggs a day. Sometimes six, which was *waaaay* more than we could eat. But too many eggs is a problem I didn't mind having!

If you've got lots of chickens laying in a bunch different spots, or you aren't always able to collect eggs every day, here's quick aside about egg food safety. You've likely heard that freshly-laid farm eggs are more nutritious than store eggs. As I understand it, they're also different in terms of refrigeration requirements.

Now, I'm very gung-ho on food safety practices, but during cooler winter temperatures, you don't necessarily need to refrigerate your hens' freshly laid eggs immediately.

Even in warm weather, if John or I couldn't get the eggs until evening, I never noticed anything amiss. From what I've read, a fresh, unwashed egg is naturally coated with a kind of "bloom" —a barrier that keeps germs from getting through the shell and inside the egg.

But if your chickens have gotten poo on their eggs, resist the urge to dunk the egg in water to clean it. Water will destroy this "bloom" and actually draw bacteria through the shell and into the inside of the egg. If you do find a dirty egg, it's recommended that you dampen a piece of paper towel, and gently scuff the manure off the shell.

Anyway, for two people who generally purchased one carton of eggs every couple of weeks, John and I could hardly believe this egg bounty! We shared dozens with my brother Ty, the Wood Guy, and with Burl, my stepdad, both guys big on farm eggs.

We usually had six or seven dozen extra in the fridge too. When a friend of John's heard about our hens, voila! We got our first regular egg customer, who happily paid $3.00 a dozen. We were like, real farmers! Then came the day John and I really dropped the ball.

The day I returned from doing errands, and found John outside...in his underwear.

7 * RED TAIL IN THE YARD

*E*arlier that day, before I left for town, I'd looked out the kitchen window at the chicken run.
And blanched.
A red-tailed hawk perched on a fence post nearby—and the girls were outside their safety zone! Then the raptor flapped its wings, swooped over the chicken compound and settled even closer—on one of the orchard fence posts.

I immediately jammed my feet into some boots and bolted outside, waving my arms. "Go on! Get away!"

The hawk lazily took off, as if not the least bit intimidated by my yelling. Meanwhile, our six hens had taken shelter beneath the sturdy Douglas fir in the orchard. And there they stayed, quaking in terror.

I returned to the house to get ready for my appointments in town. But before long, the hawk was back, alighting on the post again.

Same drill: I ran into the yard, shouting and flapping my arms. But this time, the imposing bird only gave me an insolent stare with its beady eyes. It didn't even blink. Really mad now, I picked up a chunk of wood and hurled it at the hawk. With my pathetic aim, I didn't expect to actually hit the bird, and sure enough, I didn't.

But my flimsy weapon seemed to have worked. The hawk flew off toward the deep forest next to our woods.

I figured the chickens were safe, under the tree. So did John. Still, while I was away, he worked outdoors most of the day, so he could keep an eye on them. Near sundown, he knew that any minute now, the girls would be going into the coop for the night. So he headed into the house for a shower.

Soon after that, I arrived home. I found him outside, a shovel in his hands.

JOHN'S always been the conventional type, not inclined to leave the house dressed in little more than his muck boots—even if there's absolutely no one around to see. So the underwear alone was cause for concern.

But the shovel…I felt a twist in the pit of my stomach. "The hawk?"

He nodded somberly. "I didn't get there in time."

A few minutes before, John looked out the dining room window and saw the hawk in the yard, standing over a hen. A dead one. Half-dressed, he raced out, and threw a big stick at the hawk. At least he'd had the satisfaction of driving off the hawk before it had a chance to eat its kill.

The dead chicken had been the one we never named. John had just settled the last shovelful of dirt on her mangled body when I got home.

For several days afterward, the other five traumatized hens wouldn't leave their coop. Feeling sad and guilty, John and I vowed to protect our girls a lot better. No more unsupervised roaming around the orchard from dawn 'til dusk, whether we were home or not. From now on, we would only let our chickens out of their fenced-in safety zone when we were outside too.

I learned a harsh lesson. When a wild creature "tells" you what it's going to do, believe it. By swooping in for a close look at the potential feast in our hen yard, the hawk was all but stating its intentions: it was determined to get the hearty chicken dinner ripe for the picking.

THE HAWK DIDN'T COME BACK. We like to think that since John prevented it from enjoying that delicious meal, it figured, why bother returning for another try? I suppose in the larger scheme of things, we had been lucky.

The hens hadn't been attacked by your usual chicken predators, like foxes, raccoons or coyotes—and we had lost only one. Still, I began the habit of scanning the sky as I did my chores, and checking the compost area for animal sign.

And life, as it does, went on.

8 * STRANGER IN THE WOODS

*J*ohn and I have a mid-spring homestead tradition. To get a good look at our property, we hike the perimeter of our ten acres together, in early May, before we start the really serious garden work. The woodlands are still "open"—the alders and dense thimbleberry are just beginning to leaf out, the bare blackberry canes with their razor-sharp thorns are visible against the green, and the bracken fern hasn't yet sent up their fast-growing shoots, filling in every square inch of space.

This time of year, you can actually see short distances around you and walk without tripping every few feet.

As much as I loved our woods, I never explored the wilds alone. Our woodland property is bordered by uninhabited mature forests on two sides—timber tracts—and I knew bears lived all around the vicinity. I wasn't about to risk encountering one on my own.

For a few weeks, John and I had been hearing an odd, mechanical wheezing from what appeared to be our west boundary. One day, about a week after our regular May hike, the noise seemed even louder than usual.

Like I said, no one lived back there—beyond our property was just trees and more trees. So about an hour before sunset, John grabbed his six-foot homemade walking stick and headed into the woods.

Upon his return, he met me in the garden, out of breath, his color high. "Everything okay?" I asked.

He shook his head ruefully. "You wouldn't believe what I just ran into."

HIKING TO THE PROPERTY BOUNDARY, he hadn't detected anything that might be causing the sound. Just for a change of pace, he returned through the center of our woods.

After studying horticulture in college, John is fond of native plants. And on his way back to our yard, he discovered our woods had trillium growing here and there. Finding trillium is sort of a special event, because this delicate native flower blooms only a couple of days each year.

As he bent to get a closer look at the creamy white-pink blossoms, he heard wings flapping.

"I think I startled a grouse," John told me. He was concerned the bird might have been nesting. "So I gave it lots of room and kept walking."

Going twenty five or thirty yards more, and busy looking for more trillium, he stepped on a twig.

"I heard a rustle," he said, "then suddenly, a shape moved off to my right, behind a birch clump. I peered at the clump, just as an animal turned and looked in my direction."

John took a deep breath. "It was a cougar! My heart jumped in my chest."

It was the first cougar he'd ever seen in his life. For a few seconds, he and the cat made direct eye contact. Then, "I finally spoke to it, saying something super-casual like, 'Oh, hi there!' Then I started backing up."

One thing we'd been told about big cats: you should never run away from them, or they may decide you are prey.

Walking backwards wasn't easy, he said, with all the stumps and logging slash. "But I didn't take my eyes from the cougar. After several yards I turned around, looking over my shoulder to see if the big cat was following."

He reminded himself not to run, but to walk with purpose.

"After what seemed like forever," said John, "but it was probably ten minutes—I made it inside our deer fence."

We never did discover what that odd mechanical noise was. Given the way sound bounces off the hills surrounding our place, John figured this noise could be coming from anywhere.

In any event, his cougar encounter was a stark reminder that he and I couldn't take our safety for granted.

From then on, he tucked his .380 into his belt for our woodland hikes.

THERE WERE other wild cats in the woods.

But other than that one cougar encounter, the only other big cats John and I had actually laid eyes on were bobcats. We'd spot them occasionally, padding along our fence line. Shy, and not much bigger than a cocker spaniel, I wasn't afraid of them. Not like I was of cougars.

Our nearest neighbor must have felt the same way. One day, a moveable chicken coop appeared in her small pasture, and around the coop roamed eight chickens. I admired her spunk, to let her chickens range in the open. But then, she had two dogs.

In my observation, dogs are about the best insurance you can get in the Foothills to deter wildlife. Unfortunately, her dogs couldn't keep the chickens safe. We learned a bobcat, within days of the hens' arrival, picked off four of them.

One day soon after, I was up unusually early. As I always do first thing, I scanned the yard from the kitchen window—and saw a long, low shape stalking the fence line next to our chicken pen.

The bobcat! I ran outside, shouting and waving my arms, and the animal lit for the woods. The cat didn't leave our property, however. The same week, John and I saw the bobcat outside our fence not far from the hen compound.

Naturally, the cat had plenty of opportunities to check out our hens when we weren't around. Still, I had every confidence the sturdy compound John had built would protect them. For sure, all those layers of fencing and wire must have confused the cat enough so that he quit trying to get in.

A few weeks later, from our bedroom window, I saw the bobcat again. The cat must have detected my presence, because it turned and looked straight back at me.

It was an extraordinarily pretty animal, with features as delicate as a house cat. It was hard for me to conjure up any dislike for it. Especially since the hens were safe in their cage. Besides, from everything I'd heard, bobcats posed no threat to humans.

So I put the cat firmly out of my mind.

9 * ONE MORE BENEFIT OF KEEPING HENS

Since many folks who keep hens also have a food garden, I'm taking a little detour here to talk about chicken manure fertilizer.

In my homestead-style gardening book, *Little Farm in the Garden*, I include a chapter about making compost for your garden. I mostly focus on "vegetarian" compost, made from decomposing kitchen scraps.

As garden fertilizer, it's pretty safe to apply this kind of compost at any stage of the decomposition process. I've heard of gardeners who even lay fresh veggie scraps on their beds. It seems to me you'd attract too many rodents, but apparently it works great for some people.

However, you'll probably want a different approach for manure-type compost.

With the advent of our chickens, I began keeping two separate operations: vegetarian compost and composted chicken manure. Their composition, you see, is quite different; chicken manure is highly alkaline.

Plus it takes several months longer than kitchen compost to decompose sufficiently, for safe use on a garden bed. But if you have chickens, no reason not to put all that manure to good use!

One of my favorite backyard gardening books is *Mini-Farming: Self-Sufficiency on ¼ Acre* by Brett L. Markham. The author goes into great detail about his compost-creation; it's an admirably scientific method that involves raising the temperature in his pile. This elevated temp will both aid decomposition and kill weed seeds and pathogens.

Mr. Markham's compost style has another advantage. Namely, you can put whatever you want in it!

In a nutshell, he tosses just about everything you can think of into his compost pile: leaves and veggie scraps, sure, but also weeds, prunings, paper, leftovers (including meat, dairy and oily foods, which normally you'd keep out of kitchen compost), and animal manure.

And hold on to your hat—even dead animals!

Still, his "everything and the kitchen sink" method, which actually requires extra steps like regular temperature monitoring and venting the pile, seems a bit complicated for your average time-crunched gardener.

Certainly for yours truly. While I'm all for science, I prefer my own basic process.

For my chicken compost, like my veggie compost, I keep it simple. I toss the collected manure into a pile, and mix with some kind of amendment that's high in carbon, like straw, sawdust or wood chips. I add these in generous amounts, to keep the pile from being a big old gloppy mess.

Now, if you're into math, there's a scientifically-recommended carbon-nitrogen ratio for compost-making: carbon-rich sawdust or straw—versus nitrogen-rich manure. Personally, I don't worry about specific amounts.

I simply aim to mix in lots of the carbon stuff. Whatever you add, make sure to turn your manure mixture whenever you think about it—ideally, once every couple of weeks or so. I recommend using a spading fork, which is more efficient (and easier on your back!) than a shovel.

When your pile gets too heavy to turn, start a new one. Let the manure pile sit about twice as long as the veggie compost—I give mine about a year.

When I first started a manure compost pile, I'd gotten past my fastidiousness about manure in general. Sill, I still had some reservations about how best to use it in my food garden.

After some research, I was glad I hadn't put my manure compost to wide use. It doesn't necessarily work for root crops, carrots in particular—it can make them bitter. And manure compost is especially unsuitable for potatoes, which require more acidic soil.

And despite all my exposure to manure, I'm too persnickety to use it for above-soil plants in the spring. Even if the harvest won't be for months down the road, with time for the poo to decompose, I don't like the idea of my fresh-eating produce sitting right on manure-amended soil.

In my experience, composted chicken manure generally goes best on selected beds in the fall. I've had a bumper crop of tomatoes the summer *after* I worked in ample, well-rotted manure compost the previous year.

And this compost is perfect for asparagus; again, in late fall, I will spread it on the beds. This more robust kind of compost can take all winter to decompose even further, while feeding the asparagus roots.

My persnickety-ness aside, I don't think it would harm your vegetable garden if you allowed some fresh chicken droppings here and there. In fact, I've read about hen-keepers letting their girls into their food-growing areas—seems like a bit of manure would be an easy way to "nutriate" (as sustainable farmer Joel Salatin would say) your vegetable beds.

Plus in a perfect world, chickens could fluff up the garden soil with their scratching.

Inspired by these folks, John and I actually did let our girls into our garden—once. The problem is, hens are really indiscriminate about where they scratch!

Within minutes, our girls completely plowed up a cultivated spot, disturbing some seedlings. When John and I tried to catch them, all five proved to be masterful escape artists.

After a half an hour of bird-chasing, we finally captured them all, never to repeat our hens-in-the-garden experiment again.

10 * EGG ANGST

One of the great things about keeping a home flock is that you never stop learning!

People in the know told me that a home flock would lay for several years, and live long after that—with proper care, of course.

For longtime laying, keep in mind that summer egg production is better than winter. On the other hand, commercial hatcheries keep hens in bright light 24/7, so they will lay continuously.

That seemed inhumane to me—especially when I found out commercial hens' lives are *short*.

Heading into our second winter with chickens, I noticed there was no real predictability to egg production. During the first winter with our six girls, the flock went from producing three to six eggs per day, down to one or two each day. Sometimes two or three days would pass with no eggs at all.

As late November approached, with one less hen after the hawk attack, John and I figured the egg numbers would dwindle a bit further over the cold months. I didn't mind fewer eggs for a while; the three dozen eggs stashed in the fridge would provide a nice cushion for holiday baking.

And to tell the truth, I was looking forward to a respite from trying to figure out what to do with all of them.

Having made plans to visit family for Thanksgiving, however, I had one minor worry.

"The bobcat's back," I told John a couple of days before Thanksgiving.

Turning on the coffeemaker, he asked, "Where'd you see him?"

"He was pacing along the west fence line again," I said, my gaze going automatically to the girls' run across the yard. "And here we've got our trip this Thursday."

John peered out the kitchen window too, toward their pen. "We'll only be gone one day," he reminded me. "The hens'll be okay."

I let out the breath I'd been holding. It was true—the chickens would be perfectly safe inside their safety zone. No bobcat, however determined, could squirm through our girls' secure, steer-wired cage.

When we returned, we indeed found the girls perfectly safe. But as early winter descended, we had a new problem:

Their egg production was plummeting.

JOHN and I were still giving them the wonderful organic feed—which lately had become available at our local farm co-op store—and they seemed to be eating their usual amount.

As I said, John and I expected a decrease in laying, like this time last year, and weren't dismayed by our molting birds' scraggly appearance either. Not like we'd been before. But this winter, the girls weren't only looking strange, they were acting strange.

Instead of scratching around the yard no matter what the weather, the hens seemed to go into retreat, spending most of their time in their caged safety zone. And now that there was snow on the ground, you couldn't coax the chickens into the yard for love or money.

The scratch we tossed out for them got ignored. Okay, I could understand that; plain ol' grain wasn't much of an incentive. The girls could get that any old day. But it was downright bizarre when I got the same reaction with leftover salmon bits—a treat that had previously sent the hens insane with chicken food lust.

Even more puzzling was that they were so…subdued. No brassy cackling and complaining. They spooked so easily you'd think they were purebred racehorses. What had happened to our feisty, active girls?

Even after the snow melted, they continued to shun the great outdoors to spend the days inside the coop. They'd venture out to peck at their feeder every so often, then back inside they'd go. Time to really figure out what was wrong! Were they…

*Chilly?

*Still freaked out by the bobcat that had lurked around the pen a couple of months ago?

*Or simply bummed out by winter?

By now, with the hens hanging out in the coop practically 24/7, the small space was awash in feathers—clearly, molting was going great guns.

Yet how could the girls lay if they weren't getting any natural light, sitting around in the dark all day? (I guess if I lost my clothes during the coldest time of the year, I'd be staying inside too, but still.)

Fleetingly, I wondered if the chickens were sick, but they were still eating like troopers. Whatever ailed them, by midwinter they were not only producing fewer eggs, they'd given up laying altogether.

Had they lost their mojo forever?

11 * CURE FOR THE WINTER BLUES

*T*hree weeks into the egg drought, I was getting concerned. "They're only a year and a half old," I said to John one day. We'd read that laying hens' output decreases a little bit each year. "They can't be too old to lay already, can they?"

"I always heard home flocks would lay for maybe four or even five years." John looked thoughtful. "Must be something else going on."

Soon after, I met a young gal at a writers' meeting who kept a home flock, and asked for advice. "Oh, they're just cold," she said. "Put a heater in the coop, and they'll start laying like that!" She snapped her fingers.

As soon as we got home, John re-installed his coffee-can heater from the previous winter and plugged in the light bulb. The next day, with high hopes, we checked the nest boxes. But they were still empty...and they stayed that way.

"Maybe the girls need more light," I told John. As I mentioned, keeping hens in bright light, day and night, seemed cruel. But maybe a bit of artificial light wouldn't hurt our girls for a few days.

"Seems worth a try," he replied, so I went straight out to the coop and re-positioned the light bulb, fully illuminating their roost. Now, with the inside of the coop as sunny and warm as the tropics, I figured we'd see eggs within hours…

But no. With our stash of eggs nearly gone, I broke down and bought a dozen from our local drive-through dairy stand. While I hoped my purchase would somehow prompt the chicken gods to send out some egg-laying vibes…there was still no action.

Two additional weeks passed with that 60-watt bulb burning night and day. The girls must've liked it, since they continued to hole up in the coop most of the daylight hours—even the fully-feathered hens.

Okay, maybe the chickens were simply being stubborn. Time for tough love.

EVERY DAY, I filled their feeder with balanced, no-soy organic feed. "You slackers are getting this expensive food," I scolded. "We want a return on our investment!"

John's warnings to the hens were even more dire: "Come on, girls, let's see some eggs or it's the stew pot for you!"

Joking aside, John and I actually began some soul-searching. What would we do if the hens really *had* stopped laying for good? Would we look for a new source of pullets to buy?

Or did we want to give up keeping a flock entirely? We grew so discouraged we even quit checking the nest boxes.

It had now been six weeks since we'd seen an egg. I don't know what took me so long—trying to figure things out for ourselves, maybe?—but I finally did a deep dive for our no-egg problem.

With the search prompt, **"When chickens stop laying eggs,"** the sites I pulled up pretty much told me what we already knew:

*Hens might be chilled

*Hens might be frightened
*Shorter days = fewer eggs
Then we came across something new:
*Feed isn't balanced.
Uh-oh.

"Maybe that's part of our problem," I confessed to John. "I've been cheating, mixing a lot of scratch into their feed." Apparently trying to stretch our organic layer mix with generous amounts of grain took a bite out of the nutrition they needed.

More discouraged than ever, I was ready to leave the web site...then I saw something else.

*Molting.

Reading on, I discovered the process wasn't simply to grow a fresh set of feathers. Molting also serves to give their reproductive systems a little break.

Allowing your backyard flock to naturally wind down their egg production means they'll lay longer, over the course of their lives.

I shut down my laptop, feeling a bit more positive. It looked like things were proceeding normally—and surely, once our hens' egg-producing innards were rejuvenated, they'd get back to laying. Could there be hope after all?

THE NEXT MORNING, the last day of February, I went out to feed the chickens (with 100% feed, by the way). Just for the heck of it, I checked the boxes.

And what do you know: in a nest lay one medium-sized, lovely brown egg. "John," I called, bursting into the house. "We got an egg!" We were as proud as if we'd laid it ourselves.

The next day, there was another egg, and two days later, a pair more. For insurance, we kept the light running another week, but clearly, we were back in the egg game.

12 * BAD TOADSTOOL

I was discovering yet another aspect to chicken-caring: the ebb and flow. Everything would go smoothly for a while, then not. Soon after, you'd see another rebalance. You just had to get accustomed to a bit of a roller-coaster ride.

It wasn't long before the girls were once again laying two to four eggs a day, and John and I were powering down omelets and egg salad again. Along with their egg-laying talents, the hens also regained their personalities and energy—back to scratching rain or shine, cackling and squawking whenever they heard John or me outside.

It didn't last long.

By mid-spring, as the gray and sodden April days dragged by, the hens seemed to have gotten the blues again. In fact, two of them looking especially peaked.

When chickens aren't feeling well, they stop scratching. Instead, they'll hunch up and stand around motionless, with their feathers fluffed out. I'm guessing it's kind of like when you curl up on your couch with a fuzzy blanket.

Anyway, after getting back on the laying track only six

weeks ago, the girls returned to huddling under cover, instead of running around the yard.

With the unrelenting rain, multiple kinds of fungi sprouted all over our place: mushrooms or toadstools in white, gray, brown and even bright orange, growing on soil, wood chips, and beauty bark. And especially on old logs.

Since our acreage was covered with logging slash in various stages of decomposition, these various fungi abounded.

When we first got the hens, we noticed they worked especially hard scratching up the soil all along their fence line. I guessed they were just trying to get at the bugs and weed sprouts just out of reach. The problem was, they were also digging up the ground where John had buried the poultry wire fence to keep them more secure.

To prevent more scratching under the fence, John collected some old logs nearby, and he and I set the logs horizontally along the fence line of their safety zone to keep the girls from creating more openings. Of course, like every log in our woods, these logs were rotting too.

One afternoon John came into the garden, looking downcast. "One of the hens died."

I dropped my trowel. "What happened?"

"I wish I knew," he said. "I only saw four girls, so I went into the coop and there she was, lying on the coop floor. Maisie or Daisy, I couldn't tell which."

"Oh." Feeling a twinge of sorrow, I sat back on my heels. Hens could sicken from any number of causes, like parasites or disease. I knew there had to be other reasons they died, that you couldn't necessarily prevent.

I remembered the dead chicken at our hen lady Shannon's homestead; at the time, Shannon had offered nary an explanation or diagnosis. Now, I drew the same conclusion I had then: a chicken can just up and die. Perhaps it's nature's way of culling out the weaker organisms.

"I did see a hen pecking at some mushrooms a couple of days ago," John said. "I wonder if they were poisonous." He heaved a sigh. "I'd better go bury her."

"At least it wasn't Chloe, Marilyn or Dottie," I said, my heart heavy. It was cold comfort, that our favorite girls had been spared. As John turned to fetch a shovel, I added, "Maybe it was just her time to go."

It's okay to be philosophical about these losses. Yet one good thing emerged. John decided it was time for another chicken compound upgrade.

13 * TROUBLE COMES IN THREES...OR MORE

*A*s Nature often rebounds, so did the chickens. As spring flowed into early summer, our flock of (now) four went back to their usual scratching and cackling and following us around every chance they got. Although we had more home and garden projects then we could manage, John envisioned some improvements that would make a real difference:

First, he wanted to prevent another hen's illness; and

Second, ensure the long-term health of our flock.

All this time, the girls' safety zone had been covered by a tarp. But after two years the plastic was full of holes and leaking everywhere. Even though it was June, we were still getting a fair amount of rain.

The whole compound was getting muddier, wet chicken manure littering the ground. Since the hens were walking around and scratching in that mud, our eggs were getting dirtier.

Since I had no way to determine that whatever was soiling the eggs was dirt or poo, I was changing the straw in the nest boxes every couple of days. Our chicken digs had definitely turned into a wreck.

I'm sure all my *Ewwws* about our dirty eggs also lit a fire under John. "What we need to do," he announced one day, "is to take down the tarp and add a permanent roof."

"Oh, I love that!" I said. "But what about enough sunlight for the girls?"

"How about we just cover half the cage with roofing," said John. "I'll keep steer wire over the other half. The girls will get plenty of light there."

John got cracking and laid in a supply of steel roofing. Using some short pieces of lumber, he raised the roofline by a couple of feet. After I helped him cut away the steer wire forming the top of this half of the cage, he affixed the steel panels.

It was many hours of work but finally, Voila! A dry chicken run! The chickens would be comfy-cozy even on the wettest days.

The newly raised roof left a small gap in two exterior fence walls. It was only several inches, between the steer wire fence and the roof steel panels. But a small patch of wire would be easy to install.

John and I would tackle that as soon as we found the time. But summer and fall passed in a blink. And then came trouble.

WITH VERY LITTLE WARNING, one of our dearest family members passed away. Her home, where John had grown up, was now empty.

Still in mourning, John had to leave our place every other week or so, to help his brother paint and do the long-needed repairs for the old house.

Just months later, John's son, living in Arizona, was in a serious car accident. He had multiple injuries and had lost mobility. So my husband once again left our little homestead—this time for six weeks—to care for him.

It was up to me to keep the home fires burning.

But I couldn't. With John away so much, we hadn't laid in nearly enough firewood for the winter. Try as I might—chopping what small pieces of wood I could find and foraging for burnable scraps—I simply couldn't keep the house warm enough.

Through those cold and lonesome weeks, I was grateful to have the hens to look after and talk to; they were the one bright spot at our homestead.

JOHN WAS JUST HOME from Arizona when we experienced a third, terrible blow: another death in the family.

Our dear one, only in her early sixties, had surely been too young to die. After our last goodbyes to her, John and I, still reeling from grief and stress, struggled to get back to our homestead routines.

Then one month after that loss, came a fourth trouble.

An epic, never-seen-before, never-even-*imagined* tent caterpillar infestation.

IT WAS the most challenging experience John and I had ever had together.

Springtime, so lovely in the Foothills, was completely ruined. From March through June, John and I battled this plague to save our orchard and berry patches. First, we had to destroy hundreds of nests by hand; then it was killing monster, four-inch caterpillars. Again, by hand.

All day long.

As July approached, we were exhausted, physically and mentally, and every other way you could think of. And this terrible plague had actually been another kind of loss.

I had lost a level of trust, that the natural world moves toward the good. That life "comes round right," as the Shaker

Hymn says. I'd lost confidence in the fuzzy kind of bargain John and I had made with nature: that we would cherish our place, look after it, and our place would look after *us*.

But there was no time to regroup from this latest battle. John and I still had to get back in the garden; the summer's weeding, planting, and harvesting was way behind schedule.

This past year, with the deaths, the accident, and the caterpillars, and all the time away from home, John and I had never gotten around to our "as soon as we find the time" chicken project: patching the small gaps below the new safety zone roof.

It was an omission we would bitterly regret.

14 * WILD CAT

Through the last, insane weeks of caterpillar combat, I had pretty much ignored the hens. John too. Sure, they got fed and watered, but I wasn't paying really attention to whatever else they were up to.

But ups and downs of Mother Nature finally gave us a break: the caterpillars eventually petered out the first week of July.

Days later, I'd just finished breakfast when all four hens started squawking like crazy. They often went off on one of these cackling choruses, so I wasn't particularly concerned. Still, to make up for neglecting them, I popped outside while John was checking email.

As I passed the woodsheds, it sounded like the birds were actually rattling their fence. What were they up to? A girl fight? That didn't seem like our hens at all.

I pulled a few dandelion greens from the side of the path for hen treats—maybe a snack would help them mellow a bit, and hurried to the safety zone. There, on the other side of the chicken pen, hardly fifteen feet away, was a large wild cat.

I stopped cold. Was it the same bobcat that had killed our neighbor's hens in broad daylight?

This animal's reputation for shyness must have been a rural legend. Because the cat locked eyes with me, and didn't even move when I yelled at it. After a long moment, it pounced against the fence one more time, as if to say, "Ha! You don't scare me!" and melted into the woods.

Then I saw the feathers.

They were all over the inside of the pen. Three hens, Marilyn, Daisy, and Dottie, emerged from their favorite hidey hole next to our woodshed complex, out into the main chicken area.

But where was Chloe?

I RAN BACK to the house. "John—I saw a bobcat at the pen!"

He rushed into his work clothes, and "weaponed up" with a Bowie knife and a loaded .380 pistol, in case the bobcat got aggressive. We sprinted back to the chicken compound.

"Chloe," we coaxed, peering around the usual hen hangouts, but there was no sign of her. Then I went inside the safety zone. In the far corner, next to the fence, a hen lay crumpled and motionless. Chloe.

I looked at John. "Oh, Honey, it got her."

John didn't speak for a moment. "How could the bobcat have killed Chloe?" His voice cracked. "From outside of the fence?"

Neither of us could answer that.

Sick at heart, John and I walked the fence line, but didn't see any gaps. "I wonder if the cat had been waiting for a hen to come near the edge of the pen," I said, my stomach churning. "Maybe it snuck his paw through the steer wire."

Hens were curious creatures. Drawn to the movement, had Chloe ventured to the edge of the fence, where the cat had mauled her?

"Whatever happened," and John heaved a sigh, "at least this predator won't be able to eat her."

I saw the sadness in his face as he went to fetch a shovel. My chest felt heavy and tight, but I forced myself to take my daily bike ride. We'd been lucky, I told myself, trying to push through my sorrow.

Our neighbor had lost at least six hens. Living in the middle of the woods, you had to expect predators, and this was the first big cat attack in the three years we'd had the hens.

My little pep talk didn't make me feel better. Our place hadn't felt the same since the caterpillar plague. Now, after the hawk had gotten one hen, and illness got Maisy, our original flock was reduced by half.

I returned from my ride to meet John by the woodsheds. He was actually *smiling*. "I want to show you something."

15 * NURSING CHLOE

I rounded the corner—and what do you know?

There was Chloe. She was standing, if just barely, on our splitting stump. Head drooping, eyes mostly closed, she was taking tiny sips of water from a little tin camp cup John had unearthed from the shop.

He carefully parted the feathers on the back of her neck to show me a bloody patch of skin. Still, it wasn't actively bleeding. "It looks like only a surface wound," John said, "and maybe she's just in shock. She might bounce back."

"Should I call a vet?" I asked him.

"It couldn't hurt," said John. "If she could get an antibiotic or something, maybe she could pull through."

John and I had sort of a "survival of the fittest" outlook for our place. As I said, our hens were farm animals, not pets. Either way, our budget had no wiggle room for chicken veterinary care.

I called a couple of vets anyway, and found one who dealt with chickens. "A bobcat attacked one of our hens," I said in a rush to the receptionist. "Is there any chance the doctor could prescribe an antibiotic?"

"You'd have to bring her in," the receptionist said regretfully. "I'm sorry."

Chloe seemed so fragile, I couldn't imagine moving her. And surely the trauma of a car ride would send her over the edge.

Through the afternoon and evening, John didn't leave Chloe's side. "C'mon, have another sip of water," he coaxed every few minutes. He'd always had a soft spot for this particular hen.

Since we didn't want to put her into the coop with the other three hens who might peck at her injury—the girls often picked at the bald spots of their molting sisters—John fashioned a little temporary coop for the night. In one corner of the orchard, under the fir tree that was the hens' favorite outdoor shelter, he arranged a steer wire enclosure.

Tenderly settling Chloe in, John said, "She's still hanging on." As I passed food and water over the fence, he set them next to her. "I think she just might make it."

"Chloe's our toughest girl," I said on our way back to the house. Ever the Pollyanna, I added, "I'm sure she'll be better tomorrow."

We never saw it coming.

16 * DOUBLE ATTACK

First thing in the morning, I hurried out to John's little shelter to see Chloe. When I reached the fir, my stomach turned in nausea.

All I found was a pile of feathers, and a small mound of entrails studded with flies. *Oh, our little Chloe...*

I ran to get John. He surveyed what was left of our hen, his face grim. Neither of us said anything, but I knew he was thinking the same thing I was.

We'd clearly *over*estimated the safety of the temporary shelter. In fact, John and I had vastly *under*estimated the determination and ingenuity of the bobcat. Did the animal snake a paw through the steer wire and kill Chloe, or climb the fence?

Still, what did it matter? Dead was dead.

"We can't let the hens out of their pen anymore," John finally said. He glanced into our orchard, where just a few feet from the fir shelter, a hawk had gotten our chicken two years ago.

"I'd better cover their exercise area with steer wire," he went on. "They'll be completely protected."

I gazed over at the other three hens, pecking inside the caged pen. They were getting older—they probably had another year or two of laying. But now that we were down to three hens... "I guess we won't be sharing eggs anymore."

John shook his head. "I'll get the shovel," he said heavily.

I never asked where he'd buried the first hen, killed by the hawk, nor Maisy, who one day had simply turned up dead. And I didn't ask now, where he planned to bury Chloe. I didn't want to know.

John never got a chance to put up the steer wire cover.

Two days later, I went outside, pulling on my muckboots to greet our three hens...and found another death scene.

The big cat had returned. It had actually climbed inside the covered safety zone.

I stared at the grisly sight before me, hardly believing my eyes. There was Marilyn and Dottie in pieces just outside the coop. Daisy lay nearby, her body intact but her head bitten off. Sickened, I dragged my eyes away and peered inside the coop.

There were feathers everywhere. The bobcat had obviously gotten through the small hen-sized door too. Had the hens been asleep when it first attacked, and they'd run into their safety zone, only to make it easier for the cat to kill them?

Our little flock, whom we'd nurtured for three years and was the heart of Berryridge Farm, was gone.

And it was all our fault.

17 * AFTERMATH OF THE KILL

*J*ohn and I had never found time for that earlier, first-priority project for the chicken pen: tacking poultry wire in the slender gap beneath the safety zone's new roofline.

As I stared around at the carnage, it seemed clear what had happened: the bobcat had clambered up the fence, slid through the gap John and I hadn't fixed, and went for the kill.

Bile rising in my throat, I left to tell John, trying not to cry.

John didn't speak for a long time. "I'll be outside... After a while," he finally said. *To bury them*, he didn't need to add. Seeing the remorse in his face, I knew he needed a little more time to face the task.

I went back in the coop, and shoveled piles of dirt on top of the remains. John stayed inside all day. And we didn't talk to each other that night. It was just too awful.

BUT THE BOBCAT wasn't done with us yet. The next day, I forced myself to the safety zone—and found another gruesome sight.

The big cat had obviously entered once again through the roofline opening, and uncovered the hen's remains.

I guessed it must have eaten its fill of the dead birds.

Then, in a sort of blood lust, the big cat had torn them up even further.

I'd seen bobcats enough that this murderous instinct seemed unbelievable. How could a relatively small animal could be so destructive, so bloodthirsty?

So savage?

I wondered if this cat was a particularly aggressive, resourceful bobcat. Had it had been hovering nearby for months, waiting patiently to strike? Still, whatever was driving the bobcat didn't matter. I felt the utter relentlessness of nature like a blow.

That day, John quietly buried what was left of our hens. And once again, I didn't ask where.

I never wanted to pass the spot, and hate it. I never wanted to know the place where the pieces of our girls lay, under the earth instead of on top of it because we hadn't taken care of them. Without saying anything to John, I took on the last hen chore, a task I didn't want to postpone.

Decommissioning our chicken run and coop.

As best I could, I cleaned up the feathers. There were hundreds of them, strewn everywhere—I couldn't get them all. Then I collected every bit of manure from the coop. I scooped the straw from the nest boxes, leaving them bare, then removed the feeder and waterer from the run.

Scrubbing the metal until it shone, I set the equipment in the sun to dry, then wrapped both in plastic bags. I set them in the storage side of the coop. And finally, I closed the door to the safety zone. We would not open the door again.

All that remained were scattered goldy-brown feathers.

18 * MOURNING OUR GIRLS

*I*n the days that followed, John was quiet, his face drawn as he went about his work. As I tried to catch up on all the postponed garden tasks, my own heartache made every chore an effort.

Like I said, I'd never been much of an animal person—and would never have guessed I could grow fond of chickens. Yet I found myself missing our girls terribly.

My heart lurched every time I passed the coop, though I kept my eyes averted. I missed the hens' companionable clucking and chatter, clamoring for some scratch, or to come in and hang out with them.

I even missed the rattle and squeak of the feeder that had annoyed me before. I'd always loved the silence of our Foothills life, but now the quiet seemed unnatural. Even eerie.

The empty chicken coop felt haunted.

"WE CAN GET MORE CHICKENS," John said a couple of weeks later, in a half-hearted kind of way.

"Sure we can." I felt ambivalent too. "But it's almost August…"

"Yeah," he said glumly. "Too late to find pullets. And nobody would have chicks for sale."

Not that John and I had ever considered raising chicks. After the cat attack, how could we bring in such defenseless creatures as baby chickens? They would only be bait for more predator incursions.

"Let's go for next spring," I said. "In the meantime, how about we try to find some local farm eggs?"

It took a fair amount of searching to locate a chicken operation in our area, and even more trouble to actually buy their eggs—the place was a forty minute drive away. Seeing the fresh farm eggs in our fridge lifted my spirits, but it didn't last.

For the first time since we'd moved to the Foothills, I wanted to get away. Our beloved Berryridge Farm, the place that had always given me such joy, now depressed me.

In my mind's eye, I could still see the sad little corpses of our hens, the feathers strewn around the chicken run. I wanted to escape from the guilt John and I both felt—that we'd let our girls down by not protecting them.

Grieving, I daydreamed of going on a spa retreat. Nothing to do but be a lady of leisure, getting mud wraps and massages. Or a trip to a tropical paradise, to lie on a sunny beach. Of course we couldn't afford a spa *or* a trip.

And there was no way I could abandon our garden in the middle of summer, with our full plate of watering and weeding. I simply didn't want to be *here*, with the endless chores and the fights with nature that seemed like we always lost.

Yet nature—the trees, the hills, the wildlife—had always been my comfort. I tried to remember that as summer slid into fall.

19 * MISTAKEN IDENTITY

Our quiet Foothills neighborhood was transforming. And not in a good way.

In early December, John and I awakened to the grinding of chainsaws and excavators working one of the slopes to our southwest. The noise was unrelenting. And here I'd been so *sure* our immediate neighborhood would be safe from logging.

A week before Christmas, the racket ceased, the landscape forever changed. This past summer, John and I had been forced to take down numerous deciduous trees due to caterpillar nests.

But alders aren't long-lived trees—not like evergreens. The purpose of alders in the forest cycle is to provide shade and leaf mulch fertilizer for baby firs. With wind and moisture, most of them give up the ghost after ten or fifteen years, just as the growing firs require more light.

Firs are meant to live for many decades. Here in the Pacific Northwest, they can live for centuries. To me, seeing the grandeur of the fir-covered hill laid bare was painful.

I admit that modern life requires harvesting trees for hundreds of products. And I know it doesn't make sense…yet to me, these trees, this clear-cut—it felt like a personal loss.

. . .

THE LOGGING OPERATION must have displaced some wildlife.

A few days after the last of the log-filled trucks wound down the hill, I spotted a big cat from our living room window. It was staring longingly through the fence, like it would have liked to nab a rabbit, but had no intention of exerting itself too much.

My gaze was drawn to its short body and bobbed tail—then I met the cat's eyes. "Oh my God," I breathed.

The animal's face was narrow and streaked with black markings, like the one I'd seen close up, a couple of years ago right outside our bedroom. Just like that cat, this one didn't look threatening at all.

If the cartoon character Tweedy Bird had seen this critter, he probably would have said, "I t'ink I see a puddy-tat."

In my mind's eye, I saw again the animal I'd found at our coop four months ago. Hardly fifteen feet away, the larger cat had a long, lanky body, and a wide, tawny-colored face, with bold, piercing eyes that stared right back at you.

The cat's expression, though, was what I would never forget. Fierce and insolent. And the brazen way it had banged against the fence was unforgettable.

In my fear and panic, I'd assumed the animal was a bobcat. After all, it had been a bobcat that had killed our neighbor's chickens. And I'd never seen any other kind of cat near our yard. Now, I realized how wrong I'd been.

What a *huge* mistake I had made.

It was a *cougar* that had killed our hens. A cougar that had had the nerve, the *guts* to climb our fence, and squeeze through the hens' tiny door, and go on a wholesale killing spree. Not a bobcatty thing to do at all.

I still get cold shivers when I think about how I reacted. I'd been told it's cougars, not bears, you should be truly afraid of.

As I mentioned, if you encounter one, do not turn away! You should keep facing the big cat as you quietly and slowly retreat.

Thinking our hens' attacker was a bobcat, I'd yelled at it, waving my arms, then turned my back and raced to the house.

All I can say is, if there's a next time, I hope I remember what *not* to do. Even more, that any cougars around here return to their former habits of laying low.

20 * NO GOOD TIME FOR A NEW FLOCK

*B*y March, warmer weather was only two-plus months away. John and I could finally make a move toward getting hens again! Ready to call Shannon, our chicken gal, I wanted to see if she or any local folks she knew would have pullets for sale.

But as soon as John went into the orchards for early spring pruning, we had no thought of fresh farm eggs, or new hens.

Or anything else.

WHAT JOHN FOUND WERE tent caterpillar egg sacs. Everywhere.

Dozens upon dozens of sacs on *each tree*. And not only on our fruit trees—sacs were rife in the woods, in every alder and birch. And each tiny, innocuous looking sac, you understand, will hatch *hundreds* of larvae.

From that day on, John and I spent hours upon hours first in our orchards, then the woods, trying to destroy whatever egg sacs we saw.

After the caterpillars hatched, just as we had one year ago, we spent our days killing every caterpillar we came across. But we couldn't keep up. Soon the critters were not only devouring every leaf in their path—they were even eating our *blueberries*.

This second tent caterpillar plague ravaging our place was far more intense and horrifying than the previous year. Trees and shrubs completely defoliated. Caterpillars climbing the exterior walls of our house, crawling along the roofs of our sheds.

The infestation seemed like it would never end. John and I battled caterpillars for four solid months, and it took every ounce of time and energy we possessed to go the distance.

But as before, around the first of July, the caterpillars slowly began to die off. The cocoons they had spun shriveled up; very few moths emerged. The plague really was over.

We could return to our normal lives.

AFTER THIS SECOND, even more horrific invasion, resuming our homestead routines was a struggle. Just like last summer, John and I were way behind on planting and weeding. And in the year since the chickens had been killed, their compound had gone completely feral.

The chicken yard was clogged with five-foot high weeds gone to seed, way too robust for our weed-eater. But if we were *ever* going to have chickens again, the space had to be cleaned up.

John and I gritted our teeth and geared up: pulling and whacking at what we could by hand. It was sorrowful work—we came across many more feathers.

Although the caged safely zone was as choked with weeds as the yard, we left it untouched.

"We can save that mess for another day," I said to John.

He only nodded. John, like me, still couldn't bring himself to go in there. Into our hen's graveyard.

. . .

TRYING to catch up on life in general, John and I went back and forth about getting another flock of chickens. We figured we would go for it "when life settles down."

It seems like tempting fate to even say it, but surely he and I would see a return to *some* kind of normality. Still, as the months slid by, I had to wonder if there *was* such a thing as "normal" life.

Another nearby logging operation started up—this one, just a short distance down our private lane. The crew would start at daylight. For hours, the buzzing of chainsaws filled my ears… and each protracted buzz was followed by a splintering sound, then the crash of a tree falling.

Then came the *real* noise: the relentless grinding of excavators. Within a couple of weeks, the entire tract—a mature forest—was gone.

When the site had been quiet for a few days, John and I hiked the short distance to the edge of the clear-cut. Just inside the tract's boundary lay a hemlock, its trunk nearly four feet wide, its needles turning rust-red.

Although I'd studied forestry in college, I'd never actually been in a fresh clear-cut. And before me lay a vast swathe of destruction—at least fifty acres of downed trees. Maybe even a hundred. As I gazed at the devastation around me, a snarl of dead trees and brush, I could feel the essence of the forest, its very soul, was gone. Nothing but emptiness.

Talking with the neighboring property owners, John and I discovered that since the logging started, they, like we, had seen more wildlife out in the open. Owls, bear, and one neighbor had two cougar sightings within days of each other.

That same week, a couple hundred yards from our house, I laid eyes on the first skunk I'd ever seen in the Foothills.

Carefully backing away before the skunk could see me, I realized what happens when you take down a forest—all the creatures in it have to find new homes. I wondered—would we find *more* cougars and bobcats ranging around our place?

Since moving to the Foothills, John and I had found plenty of cougar droppings on the road. Yet he'd had only the one encounter in the woods many years before. I'd seen a cougar twice: the one in our yard that had killed our hens, and months later, another big cat sighting on the other side of our back fence.

With this new loss of wildlife habitat in our neighborhood, I figured I should find out more about these alpha predators.

Research indicated that a male cougar in our state will roam a home range of about 50 to 150 square miles, and a female about half that. Apparently they'll take about six months to cycle through a given hunting ground—and they definitely know how to stay out of view.

When it came to bobcats, especially after my cougar wake-up call with the chickens, I'd learned to recognize these medium-sized felines at a glance. Apparently those cats are not quite as reluctant to be near humans as cougars. Now and then, John and I would find a bobcat skulking near our fence line.

One August day, we had the extraordinary experience of encountering one out in the open. As I watered our biggest blueberry patch and John worked on building a new carport, a young bobcat entered our yard. Without hesitating, it sat right in the middle of the driveway.

I went very still, then John saw it too. He and I carefully walked closer. Yet the cat didn't seem at all spooked. Our area was in the midst of a long dry spell—maybe the bobcat was thirsty and had smelled the water.

I put out a bowl of water as close to the animal as I dared, then retreated a fair distance away, hoping it would take a drink. The cat lingered in the yard, but I never did see it go near the bowl. I only hope it found water somewhere.

Still, I also had to wonder: what did the presence of these big cats mean for keeping chickens again?

21 * STILL WAFFLING ABOUT CHICKENS

A new granddaughter came into our lives. Yet as joyous as this event was, a new baby in the family meant even more time away from our place. For now, it seemed clear that another flock of hens wasn't in the cards.

After running into a lovely young woman in the village who kept chickens, we made arrangements to give her our nearly-untouched 40-pound sack of layer feed.

As the months passed, John and I continued to debate whether to get more hens. As if deciding *not* to decide. Even after a couple of years, it was painful for me to walk by the empty run—the memories of our girls' violent deaths still felt fresh.

Sometimes I imagined I could still hear them clucking.

DESPITE ALL MY SAD MEMORIES, though, one late summer afternoon I couldn't take the tall weeds in the chicken compound another second. I spent the next two days cleaning out the untouched caged run and coop.

I didn't take on the chore to prepare for new chickens—not

exactly; more to bring a sense of order to our place. Still, in my secret heart, I *did* want to have the place ready, just in case. Besides, taming this jungle felt like a real accomplishment.

As John came over to check on my progress, he was quiet. Finally he said, "Seeing this cleaned up—it makes me want chickens more than ever."

I nearly dropped the loppers. "I didn't know you still wanted chickens."

"Of course I do." He looked surprised. "I wanted to get hens ever since we lost the girls."

I didn't know what to say. I still mourned the girls and all the life they'd brought to Berryridge Farm. But were we ready to take on another flock *now*? "Maybe," I said, "we can think about getting chickens next April."

LIFE TICKED ALONG, and soon it was late fall, and I was winding down my food gardening. This time of year, save for the fir trees, the entire woodland was turning shades of tan, brown and gray. Coincidentally, the colors of the Foothills' top predators: coyotes, bobcats and cougars.

The west side of our chicken pen was hemmed in by thick woods and brush—vegetation that had provided excellent cover for the tawny coloring of the cougar—the predator that had first menaced, then killed our flock.

One afternoon John and I wandered back to the wild area just beyond the pen. We both took a long, hard look at the tangle of trees and underbrush, and reached the same conclusion.

"If we're going to get chickens and keep them safe, we'd better create a little buffer zone," said John.

I reached out a gloved hand, and gingerly tried to unwind a blackberry cane from the pen's steer wire fencing. "I think so too." Even if we couldn't stop all these hen predators from lurking near our compound, we could make sure they didn't blend into the landscape *quite* so well.

John and I hadn't done much maintenance outside our fenced areas. But a few days later, on a break from the rain we suited up, brought two pairs of loppers and a variety of handsaws back to the site and started in.

Thimbleberry and blackberry canes, some an inch in diameter, were entwined in the fencing, while a dense cluster of ten-foot saplings, vine maple mixed with young birch and alder grew only inches away.

Just beyond, a thicket of firs—a couple of young Douglas firs and a hemlock—grew on a small rise, but we left those because we liked them. And they would provide shade and protection for our future birds.

Next to all these trees and brush there was another thriving native just five or six feet from the chicken pen. We called it the "peanut butter tree," because it actually smelled like peanut butter when you sawed into it.

It must have sent out long, sprouting runners below ground, because there was another one right in the middle of the chicken yard.

Over the years with our first flock, we'd cut down that darn shrub in the yard several times. It not only kept pushing out new shoots, but seemed to thrive despite the ill treatment. All the more reason the make sure the mother shrub a dozen feet away felt the sharp edge of John's handsaw.

In any event, with John and me cutting, sawing, and hacking away at the vegetation, in several hours, we had cleared a five foot swathe next to the compound. And after going all out, we were dog tired.

Sure, we had plans to expand the buffer. But we'd take that on another day.

. . .

STILL, we were in no rush. Around this time, John and I had found a source of farm eggs, just five miles away. Throughout the winter and spring, these folks had gradually steadily increased their flock. They'd started with maybe a dozen girls milling around their lawn, adding at least fifty hens. Now, all those birds scratched near a mobile coop in a roomy pasture.

Newly stocked at the small village mom-and-pop grocery, the farm's cartons of fresh, orange-yoked eggs were easy to get, and we happily ate our fill.

It didn't last long.

Puzzlingly, each time I rode my bike past the pasture, I'd see fewer birds. Were they simply inside their mobile coop? Or had the owners moved the flock behind their new hoop house?

Then came the day I noted only a handful of hens.

We inquired about the chicken farm at our next trip to the little store. "They went out of the egg business," the clerk told us. "I heard animals got the hens."

It seemed unbelievable. Yet in the space of a few short months, these folks' dozens of hens had apparently been killed. After paying for our purchases, John and I didn't talk much on the way home. Maybe he was thinking the same thing I was...

Now *that* death toll was a good case for dropping our chicken idea.

So there we were...still on the fence.

22 * AT LAST, A DECISION

In mid-winter came two simultaneous, life-changing events.

Our eighth grandchild arrived, a quiet little guy with strawberry-blond hair. The very same day, a severe Northeaster hit the Foothills, followed by two weeks of the most extreme winter weather our area had ever experienced.

It was John who had to deal with it. Alone.

I'd left our place just hours in front of the storm to help with my daughter's newborn 300 miles away. While I was gone, John was completely snowbound and ice-bound. He spent days without power. Our lane was impassable, so he had no way to get groceries either.

After the roads opened up and I was able to drive home, John showed me his storm photos.

My eyes went wide. The ice storm had broken dozens of trees along both sides of our lane, blocking the roadway.

Thinking of all the challenges my husband had faced without companionship or help, I looked back at him, gripped by a fresh, self-reliant fervor. "We'd better start laying in a lot more winter food supplies."

"I agree," said John. "As much as we can store."

"While we're at it," and I drew a deep breath, "I think we *really* better get chickens."

"I've been thinking the same thing," said John.

"And not 'sometime,'" I added. "I mean this spring."

In that moment, my niggling doubts crept back. Bringing a new flock to a cougar hunting ground wasn't exactly prudent. Our hen compound would need an overhaul too. And John and I had more family responsibilities than ever.

Still, we had finally jumped off the fence; our waffling days were *over*. The only question was, where to get pullets?

IN THE COMING WEEKS, the snow in the Foothills' shady spots gradually melted, and soon it was early spring. Our newest neighbors, Alan and Gretchen, had been keeping ten or so aging hens for their son's family.

Encountering the couple on our lane after my return, I was impressed that this twosome from Texas was unfazed by February's severe weather. Especially when they shared plans to raise not only more chickens, but go for a half-dozen turkey poults.

Inspired by their gutsiness, I realized how much I'd been procrastinating. John and I were no closer to acquiring new flock, and *wanting* hens wasn't the same as actually taking steps to *get* them.

Since chickens were not going to magically manifest in our chicken compound, it was time to take concrete actions. Get 'er done.

I BEGAN PUTTING OUT FEELERS.

The chicken farm about twenty miles away wasn't selling pullets. (And why would they, when those pullets were their future money-makers?) My favorite farmer's co-op store was already out of chicks. So was my second. When I phoned my *third* favorite farm store and asked about chickens for sale, the clerk actually laughed. "*Chickens?* We sold out over a month ago."

And it was only April.

I was frankly discouraged. If John and I wanted a flock this spring, it looked like we would have to take on baby birds—mail order ones. Yet were we really up for all the extra effort chicks entailed? We'd have to learn a whole new skill set. *And* buy a whole new set of equipment. That wasn't all: we'd have to take on an even bigger worry about predators.

As a last resort, I tried Craigslist. Maybe reaching out to the local community could be our big chance to get fully-grown chickens, and we wouldn't have to worry about trying to raise chicks!

I did find some hens for sale in the area. Even a few pullets. Yet each posting had two common elements.

First, each post offered only *one* chicken. Even with my limited experience, I knew creating a compatible flock of hens from multiple sources was very dicey at best.

Second, and even more daunting: each post included warnings about bird flu.

Oh dear. I wasn't up for worrying about testing our theoretical new flock—and I certainly didn't want to risk bringing the deadly illness into the neighborhood, potentially affecting the new flock Alan and Gretchen had planned. Really disheartened by now, I told John what I'd discovered.

And he and I came to the same, sad conclusion.

We had no chance of getting hens, not until next spring. A whole *year* away.

23 * A WELCOME TWIST OF FATE

Two months later, I ran into our neighbor Alan, clearing the last of their broken tree limbs from the winter's destruction. As we chatted about our current homestead projects, he mentioned their turkey poults had settled in nicely.

"Say, we ordered a bunch of chicks that'll arrive in a couple of weeks," he added. "Would y'all like us to set aside four or five of them for you?"

My heart leaped. "You mean it? We would absolutely *love* to buy a few of your chickens."

"It would be no problem," Alan assured me. "We'll raise 'em for a couple of months, then they should be ready to move to your place around mid-October."

Elated, I thanked Alan profusely, then hurried home. The twists of fate John and I have encountered always seemed to bring more problems—our well going dry, a septic tank backup, and the caterpillar plague, to name a few.

For the Universe to move in such mysterious ways to our *benefit*—well, it felt like a miracle.

I found John working on his new shed. "You'll never guess

what happened!" I told him my big news: we wouldn't have to wait for the chickens we'd been hoping for!

"Wow," he said smiling. "I never thought we'd have hens this year."

"We've got so much to do first," I said.

Then wished I hadn't.

John's face turned sober. He knew as well as I did that our chicken compound, comprising the coop and caged run was a *disaster*. The fireweed and thimbleberry jungle (and a zillion other kinds of weeds) I'd cleared two years ago in the chicken yard had simply gotten reinvigorated, more robust than before.

Everything had gone to seed several times over, and now the clean-up seemed even more overwhelming.

As for *inside* the run, well, John and I had never had the heart to go back in there, much less tackle the weeds.

But if we were planning on getting hens, we really would have to start *some*time—and that sometime was *now*: Clear the weed wilderness. Redesign the roost inside the coop. Cut down the maple coppices that were threatening the integrity of the wire roof.

And most of all, add the critical fencing improvements to create a cougar-proof pen.

It's funny, that despite Alan's offer to sell us some young birds, I was afraid to hope too much.

It seemed too good to be true—that John and I could obtain a new flock of hens with so little trouble. Like manna from heaven. I know this superstition was the reason I put off whipping our hen compound into shape.

While superstitions are one thing; bad omens are another. Three weeks after Alan's generous proposal, I saw not one, but two cougars on our lane—only a hundred yards from our house.

Was the Universe warning us off? Maybe we *had* made the wrong decision, and chickens just weren't in the stars.

Alan and Gretchen were such a warmhearted twosome, I knew they wouldn't be upset with us if we changed our minds. But I couldn't imagine having a new flock *nearly* within our grasp, then backtracking.

Especially the early fall day our hen benefactors invited John and me to stop by and check out their flock.

As Gretchen and Alan gave us a tour of their poultry operation, I was nearly speechless with admiration. I briefly checked out the fishnet-covered shelter for their half-dozen turkeys, but I pretty much only had eyes for the chickens.

Ten or so older hens in a variety of breeds scratched around one pen, while adjacent to it, a second run held couple-dozen, multi-colored young birds. Gazing at them, hope and possibility surged inside me—soon, a few of these little girls would be ours!

Alan and Gretchen had two well-built coops that looked straight out of a homesteader magazine. One of the coops was a brand-new, airy, A-frame structure built off the ground, with a protected space beneath. Smiling, I watched a clutch of the young chickens wander contentedly around the sheltered "crawlspace."

A large fenced run with a few stacked straw bales gave both flocks lots of room to roam and climb. Their compound looked like hen nirvana.

"I thought I should give you fair warning," said Gretchen. "These little girls probably won't be laying until spring."

"That's okay," I assured her. "We've waited this long for fresh eggs, what's a few more months?"

When Alan proposed that we pick up our five chickens in a couple of weeks, John and I were like, "Yes!"

But after thanking our neighbors and heading home, I had doubts yet again. Our chicken set-up seemed ragged and careworn. Not new or pretty or clean like Alan and Gretchen's. And our weed-choked spots only made the whole place look worse. Still, when it came to selling us some pullets, our neighbors were clearly all in.

John and I had no more excuses.

And time was getting awfully short.

THE NEXT DAY, John drove to the farmer's co-op and purchased two sacks of the same organic feed we'd bought for our first flock. Lucky for our budget, the cost of the boutique layer mix had come down. Now, instead of twenty-five pounds of feed for the cost of a fine-dining dinner, you got forty pounds for just a few dollars more.

As soon as he got home, he started collecting tree limbs to chip, so we'd have plenty of nice clean hen bedding. Meanwhile, I braced myself, and entered the long-neglected safety zone to yank and clip the six-foot high vegetation to the ground.

Yet the weeds weren't the daunting part. Nor were the fifteen-foot limbs growing from the old maple stump.

It was my fear that I'd find years-old chicken remains.

And we couldn't introduce the little birds into a graveyard! So first, I cleared every inch of the run. When the ground was free of weeds, I peered into every nook and cranny of the coppiced maple stump, where I'd found pieces of our girls so many years ago.

My next deep breath was one of relief. I didn't find any bones.

YET LIFE CONSPIRED to delay bringing the chickens home.

As October rolled around, my days were packed with a fuller-than-usual schedule of teaching gigs and author events—activities I'd lined up back in the spring, long before Alan and Gretchen's chicken offer. Driving home from a library program,

I realized we'd made all these chicken plans, while something big slipped our minds: our upcoming trip to see the California grandkids!

Of *course* we couldn't leave our newly-arrived young chickens alone. I immediately phoned our neighbors to ask if we could pick up the birds after our return.

"That's no problem," said Alan in his easygoing way. "Y'all just let us know when you're ready."

A couple of weeks later, on the plane trip home from LA, John felt ill. By the next day he was down with a respiratory bug —*down* being the operative word. He was knocked out for nearly a week, so I had to call Alan and Gretchen and let them know we needed more time.

Then I caught John's illness, and had to phone our neighbors yet *again*.

It was downright embarrassing. After making the call, I collapsed back on the couch and closed my eyes, fretting about all the work we had to do. And after putting off our neighbors no less than three times, I couldn't help but wonder: would they think John and I weren't up to the task of looking after the young chickens they'd lovingly raised?

Were we no better than a couple of flakey, hen-keeping wannabes?

24 * TOO GOOD TO BE TRUE IS SOMETIMES...TRUE

A week before our poultry pick-up date, a Northeaster blew in, bringing five inches of snow.

We had never experienced such cold weather in early November. And now John and I had to put our chicken tasks on hold until the snow melted. With this wintry weather, I had a whole new complication to lose sleep over—the move would be difficult enough for the young birds.

How could we bring them into their new home in sub-freezing temperatures?

It was too late to back out, though; like Alan and Gretchen, we were all in. As soon as the snow started melting, John brought a ladder to the chicken safety zone and started tacking poultry fencing in the roofline gaps. Once he finished the cougar-proofing, he fired up the wood chipper and began pushing the tree limbs he'd collected into it. Soon, he created a nice big pile of chicken bedding.

Once I recovered from my bug, John and I headed to our chicken compound together.

He hand-sawed the maple coppice—while this old stump was a perfect hens' jungle gym, it had pumped out new growth for years and many robust limbs had gotten twisted into the wire roof.

Next, with all the tree branches out of the way, John made the last few tweaks to the wire roof and side fencing. An hour before we were due to fetch the birds, I brought in bucket after bucket of fresh wood chips for the coop floor and to spread around their safety zone.

Thinking positive, I sprinkled a thick layer of chips in the nest boxes too—the girls would have comfy-cozy nests for when they finally *did* start laying. At last, we were ready!

ON A CHILLY NOVEMBER AFTERNOON, John and I headed next door with a couple of cardboard boxes. Alan and Gretchen were waiting, and had already separated out the young birds for us: three black Sexlinks, one Buff Orpington, and a reddish chicken that looked exactly like the breed we'd had the first time around.

As Gretchen reminded us that they wouldn't lay for many months, I could hardly take my eyes off our five "little girls." Thank goodness, they weren't exactly scrawny. But it looked like they had a lot of growing to do before they reached the size of a layer.

My husband, who'd had a knack with hens from the get-go, managed to capture the birds with Alan's help. After a whole lot of chasing around, that is. With Alan and me assisting, John got three of the pullets in one cardboard box, and two in another.

After John secured the boxes in the bed of our old Ranger, I ventured to our neighbors, "So, what do we owe you?" We hadn't discussed the price of their chickens.

Alan mentioned a far lower amount than I expected, so John and I persuaded him and Gretchen to accept several dollars more for each bird. After more effusive thank you's, John drove back to Berryridge Farm, chickens in tow, while I returned on foot.

I found him watching over the boxes, back in our chicken yard. "I didn't let the girls out," he said. "I knew you'd want to be here."

"You know me so well," I said gratefully. As he carefully released the birds, I remembered the wild squawking our first hens had made when we unboxed them. These younger chickens didn't seem *quite* as freaked out. Still, they were too skittish to let John and me get too close.

We stepped away to let the little girls explore their new space. After some hesitation, they crept to the feeder and began to peck. Still smiling, I looked over at John. As our eyes met, I could see he was as emotional as I was—that welcoming our new flock was an auspicious moment.

I didn't know if these girls could ever replace Chloe and Dottie and the others—if we would love them as much. But I knew John felt the same quiet joy that I did.

After more than four years since we lost our sweet red hens, John and I had chickens again.

PART II

Five "Mixed Bag of Tricks" Hens

25 * CHRISTMAS GIFT

It didn't take long for John and me to settle into our former chicken-tending routine.

The little girls were nervous and jumpy the first few days at our place; they mostly stayed in the coop, even during the daylight hours. But gradually, our new quintet seemed to grow more comfortable in their new home, and before long, they came running whenever John and I headed for the compound.

I'm sure it helped that the girls figured out these new humans always bring the eats, but still. John and I liked to think they just couldn't *wait* to see us.

These young ones weren't officially *hens*—not yet. Since they probably wouldn't be laying eggs for a long while, I guessed they weren't quite pullets either. In any case, watching them, I felt a sense of *rightness*. As if this new flock was Meant To Be.

And bringing chickens back to our place felt healing too. John and I no longer felt so haunted by the absence of our first six hens, or the way we'd lost them. I can't explain it, but I had the oddest feeling about these new girls—like somehow, they had always been here.

. . .

GIVEN how readily the fivesome settled in, it didn't take long before John and I came up with names for each one. "Buffy" was the blond Buff Orpington, and the one I started calling "Red" turned into "Red Rosie." One of the black chickens had a vivid ring of copper-colored feathers around her neck, and John decided she would be Penny.

The two other black chickens were almost impossible to tell apart, and we were stumped for a while. Then, about a week after they arrived, John and I were watching the girls peck at the scratch I'd just tossed out.

All of a sudden I thought of our all-time favorite TV show, *The Big Bang Theory*—and the names of the three main female characters.

"Since we've already got a Penny," I said to John, "what do you think of Bernadette and Amy?"

He got the joke immediately. "Amy Farrah-*Fowler*?" (The full name of the *Big Bang Theory* character.) We had a good laugh at the pun, then it was back to our chores, firewood-splitting for John, and coop-cleaning for me.

WE HAD NO SOONER NAMED the five chickens when a big snowstorm heralded the start of the holiday season. Even though the garden beds were snow-covered and the soil frozen, there was no time to snuggle in front of the woodstove: the new girls needed looking after.

While I'd long ago learned it was definitely more rewarding to take care of chickens that were actually producing eggs, I soon returned to my old chicken-raising mindset: simply tending to these little chickens was the most satisfying job at our place.

As it always does, the holidays approached in a rush. Before I could keep track of time, it was two days before Christmas. As usual, after breakfast I pulled on my heavy winter duds and headed outside for my daily chicken visit.

"Hey, girls," I sang out and entered the run, shaking a quart container of layer feed. "Got some goodies for you!"

Instantly, I was surrounded by the birds, making their funny clucks, like soft little horn sounds. Their waterer had already frozen solid, and the bucket of water we'd brought out for a substitute was nearly frozen too. So I dumped out the slush and refilled the bucket with fresh water.

Concerned that they weren't staying hydrated, what with the frozen water, I hung around for a bit—the girls seemed to drink more if I loitered next to their waterer for a few minutes. And it was a fun excuse to watch them peck at their food.

Despite my gloves, my hands soon grew so cold and stiff I needed to head back inside. Before I left, on impulse, I opened the man door of the coop and peered inside—part of my mama bear persona, to make sure everything looked okay.

I noticed something different—a hollowed-out spot on the floor, in the darkest corner of the coop. And what do you know: a Christmas present was waiting for us.

There, nestled in wood chips, lay a perfect little brown egg.

26 * START AS YOU MEAN TO GO ON

*A*fter so many years without chickens, John and I didn't expect our second round of chicken-keeping to proceed without a glitch. But surely we were off to a great start…

While neighbor Gretchen told us the new chickens likely wouldn't lay for months, it seemed even more miraculous that despite the cold, we found that first pullet egg so soon: less than six weeks after bringing the flock home!

Admittedly, the laying process for these young hens didn't begin in one fell swoop. After the first small egg, John and I didn't see another for a few days. The hens took yet another break, then two eggs appeared on the same day.

A tip for you chicken folks with pullets. The combs of pullets are very small—almost hardly there. If you're wondering when your "little girls" are going to start laying, here's what John and I observed: Just as the first eggs began to appear, our girls' combs were growing noticeably bigger.

Then we noticed that when either of us approached any of the chickens, she would immediately duck down on her haunches—a hen's instinctual submissive pose.

Anyway, those first pullet eggs had shown up on the coop floor, but within a week, the new girls had gotten a clue: as one girl, then another began to lay, most of the eggs appeared in the nest boxes.

Yet as the hens' initial laying unfolded, it was obvious John and I still had a lot to learn about chicken-tending.

IN MIDWINTER, John was laid up for several weeks after some surgery. I became the designated chicken caretaker. Since our coop was as cramped as ever, I was once again the coop cleaner too, mucking it out every Tuesday and Friday, rain or shine. Checking the boxes each day, I could see egg production was still erratic, but I figured this slow start was to be expected with young birds.

Once John had recovered, I left home to visit my daughter's family. In my absence, naturally John took over the chicken care (but not the coop cleaning). The night I got home, John had a positive hen report.

"The girls have been laying two or three eggs a day," he said, looking upbeat. "We've got a good supply built up."

"It's good I'm home then," I said, "to help you eat 'em all!"

The next morning, I headed to the coop first thing, dressed in my full coop-cleaning regalia. I knew that with the long stretch between coop cleaning/poo collecting, the girls' digs would not be a pretty sight. Still, I excited to see our girls after ten days away, and even happy to resume my chicken chores.

Yet as soon as I opened the door and found 18 eggs on the floor, I realized we were Doing. It. Wrong.

NATURALLY, that big pile of eggs was discouraging. But before we get into that, there's a little something about wintertime hen-caring you might find helpful.

Keep in mind that a hens' schedule is very tied to the circadian rhythm and the cycles of the seasons. They actually have a gland in their brain that is exquisitely sensitive to light, and tracks how it changes throughout the day.

When it comes to sleeping, a hen will head into the coop right at dusk, and wake up with the first light. And as the time for the sunrise and sunset changes throughout the seasons, her sleep schedule changes too.

Where we live, the summer nights are short—in June, the hens don't turn in until well after nine or nine-thirty pm, and they're up by five am.

But in the deep winter, they'll go to beddie-bye as early as four pm, and won't be out and about until seven or eight in the morning. And as I mentioned before, a laying hen does most of her pooping while she sleeps.

During the lighter half of the year, laying hens are asleep for a shorter period, thus depositing less manure in their coop. However, my first morning home it was February. With the girls in their winter early-to-bed and late-to-rise schedule, they'd had all those nice long nights for pooing.

As the hens milled around me, I'd been trying to get psyched up for what would be epic clean-a-thon. Then I found the heap of eggs.

"What's wrong with you guys?" I asked them. "I thought you had the nest box thing all figured out!"

Clearly, if John had been collecting two eggs a day, only *some* of the chickens were using the nests. The others were going freestyle.

What's funny about laying hens, it's monkey see, monkey do. They see an unusual place where someone in the flock laid an egg? They'll figure that's a desirable egg-laying location and follow suit.

And obviously, this corner of the floor had turned into the

spot where the cool girls lay. I looked helplessly at the pile of eggs and shook my head.

You may recall my earlier passage about egg food safety: that you don't necessarily need to refrigerate your hens' freshly laid eggs immediately, especially in cooler temperatures.

But now, as I looked balefully at all those eggs, that fuzzy guideline did me no good at all. Since John and I didn't know when those 18 eggs had been laid—maybe yesterday, maybe three weeks ago—all of them, sadly, had to go into the compost pile.

The situation wasn't *all* bad, of course—with so many eggs, all five birds had to be laying! Still, after I finished yarding out the piles of manure, I told John about the 18 eggs. For both of us, the floor-laying seemed like a real head-scratcher.

"Maybe the chickens got used to seeing both of us every day," said John. "There were a couple of days I went to town, and didn't visit them. And with you gone, there was a definite break in their routine."

"Maybe it threw them off their game," I said. "But now that I think of it, maybe they got discombobulated because of the dirty coop."

"Hmm," said John.

"Yeah—the girls could have been so put off by all the piles, they didn't want to hop over to the nest boxes."

At any rate, our girls had developed a bad hen habit. So how to break it?

YEARS AGO, with our first flock, I'd put a beige plastic Easter egg in the nest boxes to help train the girls where too lay. Naturally, now that I needed the fake egg I couldn't find it! But I came up with an alternative: instead of collecting all the eggs in a given day, John and I began leaving one egg in a nest.

We also resumed our daily hen visits and regular coop cleaning. The egg-in-the-nest strategy wasn't instantaneous, but after a week or so, the birds were back in business: laying in the nest boxes.

I admit, there was a bit of behavior backsliding—one or more of the hens was doing some egg-eating, and occasionally sleeping in the nest boxes too. Still, John and I attributed these issues to the birds settling into their new home *and* starting to lay at the same time.

And I think it's safe to say that hens, like humans, really do need more than simply food and water. To be well-adjusted, they need routine, including regular social interaction. Also, once they're accustomed to a reasonably clean (not poo-filled) home, they don't like a mess.

With these basic needs met, hopefully chickens will remember to sleep and lay where they're supposed to, that eating their eggs is a no-no, and otherwise work best with their "peeps"!

Yet John and I were to learn this flock's behavior issues were just beginning.

27 * NEW CHALLENGES

Now our new flock had their laying routine down pat, John and I were all set for a future of smooth chicken sailing. But things did *not* work out that way.

As winter eased into early spring, we saw a noticeable difference between this group of hens and our first flock of red Sexlinks—the red hens had been mellow as the day is long.

This mixed flock of five had the *worst* startle reflex.

Surely, I thought, they had to be accustomed by now to their new environment. *And* to their new humans! But every day, as John or I approached the feeder for a refill, the girls would jump, and flap their wings in agitation, squawking wildly—as if we were complete strangers.

John and I also quickly caught on that we had to move very slowly and deliberately around these girls. Any quick or sudden move when pouring the feed or tending to the waterer would produce that same startle reflex.

Then came the day their feed sack was almost empty. Naturally, with the cost of this feed, I wanted to make sure we used every morsel! I took the large brown paper sack into the run to tip the last bits into their feeder...

All five hens went absolutely *berserk*.

They scattered immediately in a frenzy of wing-flapping, screeching a high-pitched *gobble-gobble*. They were obviously terrified. Of a brown paper sack.

"Come on, girls," I said gently. "It's okay—it's just the feed sack, see?" But they continued to squawk frantically until I removed the sack from their sight.

A day or so later, while the hens were scratching around their fenced yard, I brought a new sack of feed to the coop storage area.

Although I wasn't particularly close, apparently just a sidelong glimpse of the big brown sack set all five off again: *gobble-gobbling* as they ran in all directions, frenetically beating their wings.

A light went off. When I saw John in the garden later, I told him what had happened. "Didn't Alan and Gretchen tell us a cougar came around to their girls' pen?" I asked him.

"Yeah," John replied. "Now that you mention it, I think Alan said it happened a few times. The bobcat visited regularly too."

"Could the hens be mistaking the feed sack for a *predator*?" I wondered aloud. "I mean, it's large, and brown, and it crackles when you handle it."

"Well, they're just birds so I wouldn't be surprised," said John. "And who knows, maybe the cougar has been visiting here."

ALAN POPPED by one spring afternoon after he'd been clearing brush near our shared property line. John showed him the new shed he was building, then I said, "You want to take a quick look at the girls?"

"I'd love it," said Alan. The three of us ambled over to the chicken yard to watch the five hens peck at the fresh green weeds. "They look like they're doing great," he said. "But I knew they would."

John and I thanked him again for making our chicken dream possible, and I quickly decided I wouldn't mention the girl's minor behavior issues.

Instead, I said excitedly, "Did we tell you? We came up with *great* names for the girls! Buffy, Rosie and—"

"Penny, Bernadette and Amy Farrah-Fowler!" broke in John. The two of us chuckled. "The black hens' names are from our favorite TV show!"

"Ohhh," said Alan in his slow, Texas twang. "Y'all really shouldn't name your chickens. Or get attached to them. They're farm animals."

John and I were used to Alan's forthright manner. In fact, I always liked the way he spoke his mind. What's more, in a past life, for several years he'd managed a chicken operation. There was *nothing* John and I could tell him about hens.

I confess, though, that I felt a *leetle* deflated. Here I'd thought our names were so clever. And while these hens weren't pets to me, I cared for them…and I *was* attached to them.

Yet I knew Alan had a good point. "Anyway," I said to him, "we've already put these girls to work."

John and I told him about our ruined apple crop the previous fall—an apple maggot infestation. But this year, we were sure, would be different.

We had just started setting the girls loose in the orchard, and depending on them to put their scratching and pecking to good use, to clear out the pests in the soil.

"Sounds like y'all have a good plan," said Alan.

Using hens for pest-elimination was just the kind of all-natural solution that I could really go for. And this flock of five were champion ground-scratchers. I don't see how even the itty-bittiest insect would escape them.

. . .

A FEW WEEKS into our orchard pest-clearing, John and I began to have doubts. But first, here's a little background into what we were up against.

The apple maggot pest is a moth that lays eggs on the fruit. From those eggs hatches larvae, aka tiny worms, which tunnel into the apple. The worms then leave behind unsightly and dare I say, unsanitary brown trails inside, called "frass." (The brown is guess what: the larvae's waste.)

As I understand it, after the harvest, the larvae enters the pupa stage. The pupa drop to the ground and overwinter beneath the fruit tree, safe in the soil. Then the moths emerge from the pupa in the spring. We were counting on our girls to scratch up every last one of those little buggers.

So we had a "job" for our farm animals. But our mixed flock actually did it a little too well.

The girls had not just scratched, but excavated sizable divots all over the orchard, some up to eight inches deep. And under the apple trees, where I assume was target-rich territory, they'd dug even deeper.

Buffy, the blond hen, was especially fond of lazing away the afternoon under one of the Honeycrisp trees. First, she'd do her dust bathing in one of those holes, then she would dig a little deeper to hunker down into it.

Between her scratching and the others', before long, the roots of all our Honeycrisp and Queen Cox trees were exposed. The Early Mac, which had never really thrived due to apple scab, was really hurting. The girls had dug so hard and so deep beneath the tree that the main roots stuck out of the ground.

Even with only gentle pressure, the poor little tree was so wobbly a good wind could topple it over.

The solution was, of course, to ban the girls from the orchard, and simply confine them to their chicken yard.

But John and I soon became uncomfortably aware that

penning up all five birds in a much smaller space was *not* going to work.

28 * BAD BEHAVIOR

I can't really pinpoint how the trouble started. The real problem was, I had no idea how to make it stop.

Our five chickens were not only a flock of mixed breeds; they had distinct personalities. The three black Sexlinks were the stronger, gutsier birds. One of them soon became the alpha hen, who made sure other girls knew who was running the show.

Rosie, the red hen, was sort of middle of the road, while Buffy, our one Buff Orpington, was a breed known for their gentle natures.

The balance of power, then, was destined to go out of whack.

The flock, early on, separated into two camps: the three black hens in one, and Buffy in the other. Rosie sort of floated between the two. It seemed to me the conflicts began sort of innocuously: after I filled the feeder and the girls came running, the biggest black hen would chase Buffy away from the food.

The easy solution was for me to hang around, and make sure that Buffy got her turn. Yet all too often, the black hen—I think it was Penny, but honestly, we couldn't tell the difference between the three of them—would chase Buffy away even when I was present.

And Alpha hen Penny (ungrateful girl that she was, after being named after our very favorite character) would continue this behavior despite my scolding.

Buffy would not or could not stand her ground—and was chased off every time. And the problem with gentle hens is that in my observation, the more they're bullied, the more submissive they become.

Soon, all three black hens were chasing Buffy from the feeder, raucously scolding all the while.

When it comes to eating habits, hens are grazers. They'll eat steadily for a few minutes when you bring in the feed, then move on to other activities. Throughout the day they'll return to the feeder every so often to nibble. It wasn't long before the black hens would know when Buffy had snuck back to the feeder—and the trio would instantly head for the pen to hassle her.

Rosie, in her turn, didn't stay neutral for long. Since even a bird-brain could tell being on Buffy's side was a losing proposition, Rosie joined up with the black hens.

Now, it's not uncommon for hens to bully other hens. But our problem wasn't only the numbers, four against one. It was also that poor Buffy was instinctively a scaredy-cat.

John and I, hearing the ruckus, would often have to leave our outdoor tasks to chase off the others, then try and give Buffy time alone at the feeder. Still, breaking up chicken conflicts wasn't how we wanted to spend our precious chore time!

Sadly, this chasing and general hassling of Buffy soon degenerated into something more serious.

The four hens started pecking her. All at the same time.

. . .

"The girls are going to need more room," John said one day, after breaking up yet another girl fight. Temporarily banned from the orchard because of the digging, the five of them were limited to their only other ranging area, the fenced chicken yard. Which they'd scratched up something awful.

"Looks like we'd better finish our big clearing project," I said glumly.

The spring before, John and I had created the five-foot buffer I mentioned—a band bordering the west side of the chicken compound. We had started our project while the woodland vegetation was still dormant.

But it was summer now, and hacking at fully leafed-out brush and trees in their robust, summer growing stage was *work*. The bracken fern was fully grown as well, most stalks five feet tall or more. This time of year, if you wanted to go into our woods you didn't walk in, you'd have to *wade* in.

Still, John and I set to it.

We had previous cleared large areas of our woods by hand for more orchard spaces. For this project, to expand our buffer into a much larger area, we knew what to expect: sawing down saplings and mature trees, and clipping dense thimbleberry and wild blackberry canes. This way, we hoped some grasses and broad-leaf weeds could start getting established.

To help the process, one of the bigger chores was to dig out another native, Oregon grape. Bees apparently love their yellow flowers, but I didn't care for this plant's invasiveness: its sharp-edged foliage covered the ground like a thick, skin-irritating carpet.

It took well over a week to clear the desired spot—about 2,000 square feet—but John and I were motivated: the girls would have a really large space directly west of their fully enclosed safety zone. In fact, John called this new spot "the West."

And now that the fivesome had a pasture of sorts, I decided, they would be *real* free-ranging hens! Additionally, the new space would be an open spot between the dense woods and the compound. If a cougar was going to lurk at the fence line right next to the coop, it would now have to do it in full view.

While I finished digging out the biggest patches of Oregon grape, and yanked out the last of the tall bracken fern, John strung a new fence of sturdy, four-foot steer wire to enclose the new area. For the final step, he began to disassemble a small section of the safety zone's fence line to create a hen door directly into the West.

At the end of the afternoon, John called, "Do you want to come see?"

Setting down my hand fork, I hauled myself to my feet and ambled toward the coop. Looking pleased, John showed me the wee sliding door he'd fashioned.

Demonstrating it, he indicated the small "handle," and how, with a long enough stick, you could open and close the door from outside the fence. "It's more like a little hatch than a door—what do you think?"

"I think it's amazing," I said, grinning back at him. "Just perfect!"

Really, it was, a total win-win: ranging in this much bigger space, the girls would have lots more weeds and bugs to eat, and they could scratch and maul the ground to their heart's content.

"And hopefully," I added, as I gave the little hatch a try, "is that the four girls will be too busy feasting on bugs to go after Buffy."

AS IT TURNS OUT, they *weren't* too busy to hassle Buffy.

We found ourselves herding hens several times a day. We'd secure Buffy in the run and close the door, and get the others in the West. But they didn't have any feed or water in there, nor access to the nest boxes.

All too often, you'd hear one hen or another making distressed sounds, as in, "I have to *lay!*" Once allowed into the run, she would make a beeline for the coop.

The whole rigmarole became very complicated! To let the four hens have access to the feeder, waterer and next boxes, I would first let Buffy out into the chicken yard, closing the door for her safety. Then I'd herd the other four in the West through the hatch and into the run to eat and lay. Then shoo them through the hatch again, into the West.

Back and forth, all through the day.

The garden, wood pile and other chores began to suffer. Instead of enjoying these hens, the four bullies began to annoy the heck out of me. Even calm, peaceable John was losing his patience.

Then came the day Buffy began to molt.

29 * HEN MOLTING MADNESS

*B*uffy had been a bit of an outsider from the get-go.
With all the hassling from the other birds, for months she'd been keeping her distance. She had always been very skittish around John and me too—and all too often, she wouldn't come near either of us.

But molting was a whole new game. And sadly, began a whole new cycle of bullying. Remember the molting process I mentioned earlier? It's when laying hens lose a large portion of their feathers and grow new ones.

Sometimes they even get bald patches. But it's nothing to worry about; this loss of feathers is just part of a laying hens' natural reproductive process.

With Buffy the first to start losing her feathers, the other hens began pecking at her thinning spots. She had already been sort of a "weak link," but now, she was constantly under attack. John and I began to wonder if the other hens saw her as not just an outsider…but an interloper.

Like I said before, it's not uncommon for a hen to bully other hens. And hens often peck on another molting hen. But poor Buffy had four aggressive hens—already accustomed to pecking her—stepping up their game to hit her thinning spots.

And not only that, the four bullies were also ganging up on her to pull out even *more* feathers.

OVER THE NEXT MONTHS, as Buffy's molting wound down, the bullying sort of stabilized. One day there would be some bullying, other days, not too much. The other hens began their own molting, and either became less aggressive, or pecked on each other.

ll these months, John and had to intervene a *lot*—once again herding chickens around between their run, their fenced yard, and the space in the West. And frankly, all this extra work was not only irritating, but stressful.

It was difficult for both of us, having to be always vigilant, on constant alert to make sure Buffy was safe.

At the same time, though, Buffy was learning to cope. She proved to be a masterful escape artist, extricating herself from the pecking, then scrambling away. However, our gentle hen paid a heavy price for playing it cool with her four flockmates.

The other hens' torment of Buffy began to step up again.

And one day, they launched the worst attack of all.

30 * IS BUFFY DEAD?

I thought they were going to kill her.

Cleaning the main hen run, I heard a terrible squawking. The four chickens had Buffy pinned against the fence, pecking at her mercilessly. Running at the scrum of birds, I shouted, "Get off! Get off her!" For one horrified instant I watched Buffy go limp, her head drooping onto the ground.

John raced over from the woodpile, reaching the birds first. "Stop that!" he yelled, pushing the four girls off Buffy.

"Is she dead?" I asked, panicked.

"No," he said, just as Buffy moved a tiny bit. She slowly got to her feet, apparently uninjured, except for losing some feathers.

As John and I chased the other birds away, Buffy ran into the coop and disappeared inside. And there she stayed.

After this most brutal assault, Buffy wouldn't leave the coop. Too terrified to come outside, she wasn't eating. Nor was she even drinking any water.

After locking the four attackers in the main hen yard, separating them completely from Buffy, I would open the man door to the coop, and coax, "It's okay, you can come out."

But Buffy still wouldn't leave. She simply milled around on the floor.

AFTER SEVERAL DAYS without eating or drinking, without sunlight or being able to scratch, Buffy was not only losing her hen vitality. She began to look ill.

She was covered with bald patches. Her comb was pale and flopped over, with strange blue spots on it. On the fourth day of Buffy not taking any nourishment, I said worriedly to John, "I wonder if she's going to make it."

John looked bleak. "There's not much we can do—we can't guard the coop and run 24/7."

We talked a little about building a separate run and tiny coop for her. But our budget had been recently stretched when we had to replace our generator, costing nearly $6,000.

Besides the expense, we were dealing with some family problems too. At this point, neither John nor I had the time or energy to take on this new chicken project, for a situation that might only be temporary.

In the short term, all we could do was hope that Buffy could hold on until some of her feathers grew back in.

THE NEXT DAY, I decided to try something new. I locked the other four hens in the West.

We had done this before, but if you can believe it, on the outside of the pen, the four aggressive hens would pace at the fence line, squawking to get at Buffy.

This time, I went to the caged run, opened the people door of the coop and left it open, blocking the view of the other hens. I sprinkled some feed on the ground in the doorway then backed away.

Buffy just looked at the food for a while. Then, low and

behold, she slowly approached the doorway. With the other hens, and me, at a safe distance, Buffy began pecking at the feed.

She didn't eat for long, and returned to the darkest part of the coop. But I kept trying.

Each morning I'd open the door, sprinkle some feed on the ground. Each time, she ate a little bit more. But she still wouldn't go near the waterer. I'm guessing the feed contained enough moisture to keep her from dying from dehydration.

A few days of this, I started to sprinkle more feed further away from the doorway, like a little Hansel and Gretel trail of breadcrumbs, to get her closer to the waterer and the feeder. And each day, she would creep out a bit more into the run.

The one day, what do you know! She went to the waterer and drank, then straight to the feeder.

I could see she was still weak. But with each day that passed, she ate and drank more, and began looking a little stronger. Eventually she entered the main yard, into the daylight. She really was going to make it!

Interestingly, during this time, Buffy lost her fear of John and me. We were able to approach her, and even get quite close, to give her scratch or to clean the coop, and she didn't skitter away.

I guess she finally figured out *we* weren't the threat she needed to worry about.

31 * BUFFY'S RECOVERY

She slowly began to heal.

Buffy's behavior returned to something closer to normal hen stuff. She began leaving the coop, going into the main run with the others. They still wouldn't let her alone, yet their attacks were far less savage.

Buffy found a way to cope once again—resuming her escape artist strategy. This time around, she would leave the coop and all but *fly* to the big leaf maple stump in the caged run.

Parts of the three-foot tall stump were decomposing, so there were only a few spots large enough for her to rest on. But the root maple was still very much alive, pumping out long, leafy branches—perfect for hen cover.

We'd find her there early in the mornings, and she would hang out there All. Day. Long. Once again worried for her health, John and I began leaving little piles of feed on her perching spot on the stump, along with a small cup of water.

This went on for weeks.

Still, Buffy was continuing to regain her health. Although her comb appeared to be permanently damaged, her feathers were growing back. She seemed to be eating all right as well.

And once in a while, if we had locked the other four into a different yard, she would leave her perch for a few minutes to scratch in the dirt. All good.

THEN ONE EVENING, I was checking on the girls when I saw an extremely unwelcome sight: three sizable gray critters streaking from Buffy's stump.

Rats! *Of course* they'd been attracted to the feed John and I had left for our hen. We had obviously "solved" one problem, only to create another.

We kept the chickens' feed in the storage shed adjacent to the coop, in a double-layered plastic garbage bin. After we found bite marks in the top of the bin, *and* I saw rats in the woodshed nearest the coop, I threw up my hands in frustration.

"John," I said, returning to the house, "I'm ready to go nuclear on these rats."

He looked surprised. *"Poison?"*

John knew I was passionately opposed to using chemicals around our place. Especially pesticides and other toxic compounds. Some years back, we'd had a serious rat infestation in our pole building shop. It was a large space, where John not only kept his many hand and power tools, but had a huge workbench for his handy-person stuff.

The shop was also where he stored *scads* of family mementoes. We ended up dealing with the rats via traps and completely decluttering the place—working from dawn till dusk for several days.

But I didn't have the time or energy to go through all that a second time.

John dutifully purchased rat poison, and set some in the storage shed, and in the woodshed where I'd spotted the rat. Over the next week, we noticed something(s) had nibbled on the poison, and at the same time, and we didn't see any rodent sightings.

It looked like the nuclear option had worked. But after a week, I also found a dead towhee bird in the woodshed.

Instantly, I was *done* with poison.

THEN, over the next weeks, something changed. No, two somethings.

Small eggs, much lighter in color than the other eggs, showed up in the next boxes. It looked like after all these months, Buffy had begun to lay again!

Interestingly, the four other hens began allowing her to eat at the feeder. I wonder if Buffy was exuding some new kind of hormones/pheromones, which other birds sensed—which now made her part of the flock.

Interestingly, as she rejoined the flock, Buffy returned to being skittish with John and me. She wasn't as frightened of us as she was before the attacks, but now, when we offered her a nosh from the feed container, she wouldn't eat from it like she did before.

I missed that little connection with her. Yet it was a huge relief, knowing that Buffy was healing: eating, drinking and generally regaining her chicken mojo. And with the additional ranging area in the West, John and I got a respite.

Now that the Gang of Four had wound down their bullying, it seemed safe to let all five out there together. All the hens were really happy in this spot: lots of leaf mold and forest duff to scratch in, the big firs for shade in hot weather, and rain protection too.

John and I got into the habit of just leaving the hatch open— just wide enough for a hen to squeeze through. This way, any girl could come and go at will, for food and water, *and* have access to the coop for laying.

Soon, we got even more relaxed about the hens being back there. We would leave the hatch open overnight, and any hen could go out and free-range as soon as she was awake—which was long before John and I were up and around. The stress and pressure of herding hens, the in-and-out routine, finally began to ease.

NATURE ABHORS A VACUUM, as we all know. Around this time, new, non-chicken worries created fresh stressors for John and me.

I had mentioned family problems...one beloved member was in the middle of a nasty divorce, which also involved four children including a toddler and a preschooler.

Our support was needed, including many trips out of town. And not knowing how else to keep Buffy from getting attacked by the Gang of Four in the locked-up run, we left the hatch open.

Yes, John and I knew letting the hens out in the West all day long wasn't a long-term solution. Especially since we could never predict if the bullies were going to attack Buffy any given day—or would leave her alone.

But we were at our wit's end about the whole situation: two years with this mixed bunch of hens, and their flock dynamics still hadn't stabilized.

From what I know about roosters, a male chicken could look after the hens and keep them a little more organized. For instance, a rooster will often usher the flock into the coop at bedtime, and out of the coop in the morning.

Maybe a rooster for our flock could prevent the ganging up problem; an alpha male could certainly provide some protection from outside predators.

But I wasn't up for the crowing all day long—and I'm sure our neighbors wouldn't like it either.

As for Buffy, with her fragile health, how would she cope with a rooster's mating behavior? I understood it was sort of a rough business. So acquiring a rooster didn't seem to be any better of a solution than leaving the hens out all day long.

At any rate, John and I needed a break from babysitting hens—and we took one: a trip out of state to celebrate our granddaughter's 11th birthday. Our kind neighbors, Alan and Gretchen, experienced chicken-keepers who had raised these girls, offered to look in on the hens.

Every time I've had to leave our place, I always gaze at the forested mountains until they disappear from sight, saying a silent goodbye. But for this trip, as we drove down our lane, I didn't spare my beloved Foothills a backward glance.

For a few short days, I just wanted to *not* worry about chickens.

32 * AN OMINOUS SIGN

*I*t was near midnight. A chill November night.

John and I pulled into the driveway, happy to have had a wonderful family visit—and delighted to be home. Weary from the long day of airports and travel, I grabbed my duffle bag and headed for our entry gate—then stopped cold.

There was a scrap of paper attached to our gate. I *knew* something was wrong.

"Oh, John..." Grabbing the paper, I started reading in the light of our car's opened hatchback. It was a note from Alan and Gretchen.

We have heartbreaking news about your hens...

I didn't read any further. Fearing the worst, John and I rushed into the house to grab a headlamp and hurried to the coop. I lifted the vertical shutter and as John held the lamp high, we peered into the interior. It *was* the worst.

The coop was empty. Our little flock was gone.

In shock, John and I staggered into the house with our luggage. We hardly slept that night.

. . .

HEARTSICK AND WRACKED BY GUILT, I called Gretchen first thing the next morning. I heard the distress in her voice as she told me what had happened.

The day after we left, Alan had stopped by our chicken compound to say "hi" to the girls and top off their feed. Instead, he found three of the hens had disappeared.

The fourth one was on a nest, dead. Buffy was still alive, cowering in the coop.

Alan took the dead hen away to bury it, and by the time he returned, Buffy had vanished too. "Sue," said Gretchen in her soft Texas accent, "We feel so bad. I mean, it was on our watch—"

"Oh, Gretchen, please don't." I felt beyond awful. "What happened was totally our fault. I'm just so, so sorry you had to deal with it."

I could tell she still felt terrible, no matter how much I reassured her. As she and I tried to piece together what animal or animals might have done it, Gretchen said, "The strange thing was, the dead hen in the nest showed no sign of an injury."

"I wonder...if she died from fright," I said slowly, picturing the terror the birds must have experienced.

"Maybe a heart attack or something," said Gretchen. "We lost three of our birds like that, dying from no apparent reason."

"But our other four girls..." My voice trailed away.

"I suppose it could have been cougars," she said. Gretchen knew quite a lot about the local wildlife; her son was an avid outdoorsman and hunter. "Most of them carry away their prey to eat in privacy."

I didn't want to remind her that a cougar that had killed our first flock—and had torn the chickens apart right there in the pen. Instead, I thanked her again, for all she and Alan had done for us, and said goodbye.

Talking with Gretchen, and hearing her gentle Southern accent had been comforting.

But there was no escaping the next step—trying to figure out exactly how this second flock had been killed.

AFTER MY PHONE CALL, John and I donned our work gear and headed for the chicken compound. Checking the nests, we found two pristine eggs. Then steeling ourselves, he and I rounded the corner of the coop and entered the caged pen.

There were no bodies, no chicken parts strewn around, no carnage like the last time, when a predator attacked our first set of hens.

Feathers provided what little evidence there was: a cluster of black feathers caught in the safety zone's fencing next to the woods, and a pile of white-blond feathers—Buffy's—at the bottom of the ramp into the coop.

Taking a deep breath, I opened the man door into the coop. We found more feathers on the floor, but no corpses, no blood. The animal or animals had carried away the hen's intact bodies.

"And look," I said to John. "There's hardly any manure on the roost." I'd cleaned the coop the day before our departure. "This attack had to have happened the morning we left."

Returning to the pen, we looked around a little more, John mostly silent. The waterer was still completely full, as was the feeder.

The animal had likely gotten to the birds shortly after we'd driven away. But whenever the killing began, the suffering and death of our hens was our fault, plain and simple.

After I removed the waterer and feeder and emptied them—we didn't need any more reminders of our girls—I gazed at the woods on the other side of the pen. I made myself face how very negligent John and I had been.

Instead of locking the hens into the caged run, we'd left them vulnerable to any and all predators coming through the hatch from the West.

John and I had all kinds of excuses for keeping the hatch open. Buffy would be safer from bullying, and the advantages of her safety, we thought, would outweigh the risks. After all the months of terrible bullying, John and I were so stressed out we were trying *anything* to make the situation easier.

And so on.

But there's something I didn't want to admit before. We got…complacent. It was such a hassle to monitor the hens every waking moment. Particularly since John and I, both self-employed, had a lot of writing and office work indoors.

It's true, that he and I have struggled with what's commonly called work-life balance, between our jobs, family responsibilities, and looking after our place.

Only too often, the life part of the equation—food-growing, chicken tending, firewood chores and trying to keep the woods from taking over—is essentially *work* too. And time for actual rest is limited.

So because what felt like *more important* activities, John and I gradually allowed the hatch—the small entry into the caged safety zone and coop—to stay open 24/7.

With a heavy heart, I stowed the waterer and feeder in the shop, revisiting the last few months. John and I had gone out of town six separate times, leaving the hatch open and the hens to their own devices. And things had been fine.

Until they hadn't.

33 * TRAIL OF FEATHERS

Still hoping to identify what kind of animal had attacked our girls, John and I left the compound and entered the gate into the West.

The first thing I saw made me even sadder.

"Look at that," I said to John, wishing I could turn back the clock, wishing we'd closed the hatch before we left. "White feathers."

Buffy had clearly been carried off like the other three. There was a trail of white feathers, leading diagonally all the way through the West's enclosed area, then beyond the fence into the denser woods of our acreage.

Yet maybe, clearing this large space, John and I had provided even more predator habitat: we had carried all the brush and tree limbs and other slash we'd cut into the woods. About fifty yards from our clearing, we stashed all of that brush and wood behind a giant rotting log about three feet high.

We had so much material that we had to pile it higher than the log itself. I gazed at the tangle now, certain that any number of predators could burrow beneath all that brush to create a perfect den.

The feather trail had headed straight for this fallen log—then about twenty feet away, petered out. We found no further evidence.

Wherever the hens were taken, we would never know.

"I wonder if it was coyotes that did this," I said to John. "Remember the night before we left on our trip? A pack of them howled practically right outside our bedroom."

"It doesn't matter," said John soberly. I knew what he was thinking. Dead is dead.

John and I felt doubly guilty about our wonderful neighbors Gretchen and Alan. After volunteering to do such a lovely favor for us, they'd had to personally deal with the girls' deaths.

Additionally, since they'd raised our five girls from chicks, the couple had been invested in the birds' well-being.

After we'd lost our first hens, Gretchen and Alan's neighborliness and generosity—selling us their pullets—had brought life back to our little homestead. And somehow, with this kindness, they had also brought *possibility*.

John and I had weathered many setbacks here on our homestead. But this one—which could have been prevented—felt doubly difficult. Although this mixed flock and their bullying felt so very challenging at times, it *was* a loss.

As the gray November days passed, John and I missed our hens' companionship, and missed having animals to care for. We'd also lost some of our food supply self-reliance.

I had lost something else: my pride in keeping a healthy flock—and the contentment I always felt gazing at our girls doing their little henny thing.

Our chicken compound was straight across the yard, in full view of the kitchen window. I spend a *lot* of time at the sink right in front of that window, processing fruits and vegetables, cooking and doing dishes, so I look out that window many times each day.

Now, death had stalked Berryridge Farm a second time. My

gaze was still automatically drawn to the chicken pen. After the last two years of keeping these girls, I still searched for movement, seeking a glimpse of the hens that weren't there.

All I saw, and felt, was emptiness. With a heart heavy with regret.

PART III

Five Blonde Buffies

34 * A FRESH START

*A*fter all that happened to our last two flocks, John and I dreamed of a do-over.

The months following our loss were like no other. Our three-year-old grandson developed severe peritonitis after a burst appendix, and for many days, it was touch and go.

I stayed with the family for over two, anxiety-ridden weeks to care for his siblings. And wondering if life would ever feel normal again.

Our little man did recover, though it took him many weeks to regain his appetite and three-year-old vim and vigor. Then one month after he was home from the hospital, our lives—and everyone else's on the planet—was upended.

The Covid pandemic hit.

In the long separation from our family and friends, our garden was my consolation, and John's too. That summer was marked by a bear invasion into our orchard—shocking to us, but probably business as usual for the bear.

It nearly destroyed our crabapple tree, and we got a sense of the real damage bears could do to our place.

After such a year, as fall approached, John and I yearned for a chance recommit to our little homestead. To make a truly meaningful step forward.

And bring life back to our place.

TEN MONTHS after animals killed our mixed flock, we got the fresh start we longed for.

Our wonderful neighbors and hen benefactors, Alan and Gretchen, didn't hold the loss of the hens against us. Ever since they began raising chickens and turkeys, they too had struggled with all kinds of predators, and had lost a hen every so often.

In fact, every couple of years they had to replenish their flock of hens with new chicks.

I'd venture to say there *are* no safe chicken spots in the Foothills. But their homestead was a lot more baby chick-friendly than ours.

Gretchen and Alan's ten acres had been cleared by the previous owner, so most of their property was open pasture and gardens, free of trees and brush—with minimal cover for cougars and coyotes.

Also, their hen operation was right next to their house, *and* they had a sweet-tempered Border collie who patrolled their poultry compound.

The spring after our flock was wiped out, Gretchen and Alan brought home a new bunch of chicks—Buff Orpingtons. And when they offered to raise a few to sell to us, well, John and I absolutely *jumped* at the offer.

THESE BUFFIES really did represent a new beginning.

Now, as far as chicken-raising, our place had handicapped us from the get-go. John and I had built our homestead in a piece-meal way, one vegetable bed and berry patch, one orchard, and one woodshed at a time.

By the time we decided to bring hens to our place, four years after we began our lives here in the Foothills, we had filled our one cleared acre with—yes—vegetable beds and berry patches, orchards and sheds.

We didn't have any space for a chicken operation close to our house. As a result, we had no choice but to build our coop, caged run, and chicken yard on the other side of our main garden area.

This hen area was also beyond our complex of woodsheds and one of our orchard spaces. And ever since the loss of our first flock, I'd always regretted our girls had to live so far away.

Yet John and I, being highly motivated to get hen-raising *right* this time, decided to make more adjustments to our coop. Since we'd been dreaming of new chickens all winter, I'd been researching various coop arrangements.

I finally came across a design in *Country Living* magazine that would be fairly simple to execute.

Keep in mind our coop still wouldn't even be *close* to *Country-Living* fancy! But the basic setup featured in the article seemed very sound. And as summer wound down, we got started.

John completely disassembled the freestanding roost that had always been too large for the coop. Using two birch boughs about two inches in diameter, he created a whole new two-level roost. Beneath it, he installed a sort of table made of hardware cloth wire in a wood frame, which served as a platform for poo-catching.

As for remodeling the nest boxes, which had been located way too high, he detached them from the outside wall, and reattached them closer to the ground by a couple of feet.

The new coop design would make for easier cleaning, and the much lower nest boxes would reduce a hen's temptation to sleep in a nest! The one improvement that would make the hen compound just about perfect was the one we couldn't make:

Tear down our whole chicken operation and build it closer to our house.

THE DAY of our pullet pick-up, John and I had the girls' new digs all ready. Over the last week, we had cleared the tall weeds choking the chicken compound.

That morning, as I had done before we brought out mixed flock home, I had laid lots of fresh, sweet-smelling wood chips in the chicken pen, scrubbed the waterer and filled it with clean water, and poured fresh organic feed in the feeder.

Finally, I turned my attention to housecleaning the coop. After shoveling out all the old floor bedding, I brought in another wheelbarrow full of fresh chips for the floor and the nesting boxes, with plenty more to spread on the platform beneath their roost.

Once finished, I stepped out of the coop and surveyed our now-tidy compound, as excited as I was ten years ago: the moment we brought home our first flock.

And on this sunny September afternoon, on a day that seemed full of promise *and* possibility, John and I became the new caretakers of five Buff Orpington pullets.

35 *BACK IN THE HEN BUSINESS

*A*s you already know, that first night with our new flock of Buffies was a little rocky: they had mistaken the slippery little overhang in the run for their nighttime roost.

I had to pick them up, one by one, and move them into the coop. But other than that small glitch, the five newbies settled right in.

These young Buff Orpingtons lived up to their reputation as gentle, friendly hens. It was easy for John and me to feel connected to them, like we had with our poor Buffy—though we had tacitly agreed not to call any of the new blonde hens "Buffy" too.

All five would always come to greet us—not one would shy away. Even more wonderful, the new girls started laying regularly within a few days of their arrival.

Throughout the fall, the Buffies ranged contentedly in the orchard adjacent to our food garden. They didn't create huge holes like the mixed flock had; still, within a few weeks, they had pretty much torn up the ground into mud.

John and I weren't too thrilled about letting the new kids into the West to forage, after what happened to the previous hens. But we slowly grew more comfortable opening the hatch for a couple of hours, while John and I worked nearby, either in one of the woodsheds or at the compost pile.

However, these girls seemed happy enough to hang out in the more "civilized" spots too, either their fenced yard or caged run. The yard, which the hens had soon scratched every shred of green into oblivion, had a little stump they could jump on.

In the caged run, besides their feed and water, there was the large, big-leaf maple stump where poor departed Buffy had spent her days. These girls seemed to enjoy perching on it too, despite the jagged, decomposing wood.

It amazed me that they would somehow manage to find a way to balance their claws on the uneven surfaces.

If they wanted dry feet for a while, the girls also used the outdoor covered roost John had created years ago, and the little roof over their feeder.

Even after their mishap on the overhang that first night, these hens, like our others, spent a fair amount of time looking in the window into the adjoining shed.

We only kept feed in there, so it was an ongoing mystery what they were looking at. The mice trying to chew their way into the feed bin? Or maybe the girls could smell the feed sack better up on the roof!

As we hadn't remodeled any of the coop's exterior, the girls' setup was the same as it had been for the other hens. Next to the slippery overhang we had a typical hen door: a small ramp leading up to a hen-sized opening cut into the coop wall.

A few inches away, a "people" door led to the inside of the coop. It's funny, that with all the hens at our place, even if the big door was wide open, they never used it. Instead, they would always ascend their little ramp to enter the coop, and exit the same way.

If, despite all these features, they wanted something to break the monotony, there was the thrill of John (or the Rooster, as I called him, since he's the only male on the place) spoiling them. Every morning, he'd go out first thing to toss them some scratch.

After the young lady at the feed store told me scratch grains are like hen candy, I had to keep an eye on my husband so he didn't give them too much!

We also found that overdoing the scratch seems to upset their tummies a little—maybe too much fiber. Whatever it was, after the girls over-feasted on scratch, coop cleaning would turn into a far more unpleasant chore than it needed to be. If you get my drift.

So John and I settled back into our hen-caring routine as smoothly as the new girls adjusted to their new home. One thing we didn't do, though, was give each hen a name.

36 * CHICKEN LOCK-OUT

One afternoon in early January I was finishing up my winter chores. As always, I focused on my most important task: checking the hens before they turned in for the night.

You may recall the light-sensing gland in their brain I mentioned. What's entertaining is that you can pretty much tell time from your laying hens! Rain or shine, they'll turn into their coop to sleep exactly at dusk, no matter what the season.

Hens are all about routine. About fifteen minutes before beddie-bye, they will generally dial down their perpetual foraging—which I suppose is a nice word for the way they tear up the ground!

The Buffies constantly created big holes all over the cage and yard; they were especially efficient with moving piles of the mixed dirt and wood chips from one spot to another.

For some reason, they almost always created a mound of it in an inconvenient spot: near the people door into the caged safety zone.

Typically, during this fifteen minutes, the girls would

wander into this caged pen to mill around their waterer and feeder.

I would talk to them, ask them about their day, and shake their feeder to redistribute the grains. I always agitated the waterer as well, to encourage them to get a sip or two.

Laying hens, in my experience, tend to get kind of cranky before bed—I wonder if it's some kind of hen anxiety about getting the best roosting spot in the coop. So I would leave the people door into the pen partway open, in case any girl wanted to go back out into the yard for some last minute dirt-scratching.

Or, as our little Dottie did in days gone by, in case one wanted to come out and socialize with us before turning in.

Once I'd completed this brief bedtime routine, I would leave the compound to toss the day's kitchen scraps on the compost pile nearby, and chop some firewood in the shed just next door. Then I'd take a two-minute walk down the lane in the last bit of daylight to work out the kinks from wood-chopping.

By the time I returned, the girls would always be on the roost, so I could secure the pen for the night.

But on this early evening, things went down differently.

I WENT to the pen to close it up, and found the man-door already shut—and a mound of blond creatures huddled up right up against the door. They were hunkered down so tightly they appeared to be one large bird.

All five girls, instead of staying in the caged run, had, for some unknown reason, gone back into the yard. And somehow they managed to push the people door closed.

I blame all the dirt they'd shoved around the entryway. The result?

They'd locked themselves out!

Now, hens aren't shy about complaining when something

isn't right. But I didn't hear them kvetch because I'd been just down the lane. So the girls did the next best thing to roosting: they piled in together into the dirt to keep warm and secure.

All five seemed fast asleep, although they couldn't have been hunkered down there for more than a few minutes. To rouse them, I said, "Hey, guys, wake up."

No result. I prodded them gently with my hands. "Come on girls, wake *up*—you don't want to sleep outside all night, do you?" (And be food for bigger critters?)

With my touch, one girl sleepily shifted out of the mound, then finally a second one. But the other three ignored me.

With two less hens in the mound, I was able to open the door a little, but neither of the two hens *got* it—that they now had a pathway into the coop.

Now, every instinct should have told them to get inside and roost as usual! But they were too discombobulated to even take a step around the door and enter the pen.

Apparently it was up to their human to set them straight. I opened the man door of the coop. Then, just as I'd done the first night, when they'd decided to go to bed up on the overhang, I began ferrying the hens, one by one, from the yard, through their run into the coop, then finally onto their roost.

The two semi-awake hens were compliant enough to let me grasp them. But the others? No way! They flapped their wings, trying to get away, *buck-buck-bucking* all the while.

It was clear that once hens turned in for the night, they did *not* like being messed around with.

The last hen in the mound was nestled in the dirt—like *right* down in it. And oh my gosh, she had a proverbial *cow* when I extracted her from her little nest.

As I carried her into the coop, there was much agitation and kvetching and to-do-ing from the flock. There was even more as they got themselves positioned onto the roost—in the correct pecking order, I assume.

At that point, all five seemed to dislike me very much. (After all I'd done for them!)

The next morning, I wondered if the hens would still be mad at me. Or worse, be afraid of me. But they were back to their usual sunny dispositions. Apparently no harm done, except that I felt very guilty for upsetting them.

My big takeaway from this experience: I always made sure that pen door was wide open at bedtime, and the doorway cleared of that day's dirt piles!

37 * AN UNFORESEEN DEVELOPMENT

With our new flock, John and I had hit the jackpot. Or so we thought.

For months, our five Buff Orpingtons were model chickens. Aside from the two bedtime glitches, they'd quickly settled into their new home. As I mentioned, they also started laying right away, and were cooperative and copacetic.

A far cry from our previous flock.

One of the hens, as is typical, became the Alpha girl—the one who seems to set the agenda for the flock. Our new Alpha wasn't really aggressive, thank goodness. But strangely enough, she was the smallest hen!

Anyway, we thought we had it made. That is, until mid-spring—when one of the hens went broody.

Broodiness is when a hen's mama instinct kicks in, and her only focus in life is to sit on eggs to hatch them. I had always heard Buff Orpingtons are especially prone to it, but Buffy, from our second flock had never gone broody—probably because of the bullying.

Anyway, when one of our new blonde hens wouldn't come

outside anymore, I suspected broodiness—and a little research confirmed it.

Whether there are any eggs beneath her or not, a broody hen will sit on the nest in a sort of somnolent state, from sunrise to sunset. I suspect with that kind of dedication, the hen's hormones have sort of tricked them into thinking they *are* hatching eggs.

It's like she's mostly asleep—but if you try to get her off the nest, she'll hiss big-time at you.

There are two problems with broody hens. One, she stops laying eggs. And bear in mind that even if she's not sitting on her own eggs, she's all too willing to sit on the other hens'.

The second problem is that she will seldom leave the nest—not even to eat or drink. Which can lead to a broody bird's insufficient intake of food and water.

From the day we'd brought the flock home, this particular hen who wouldn't leave the nest had seemed to be less vigorous than the others. She had also developed her hen characteristics somewhat more slowly—her comb was sort of shrunken, and pink instead of a pale red.

On the day I discovered her sitting on the nest all day, the day she refused to move, I took charge.

I lifted her off the nest, and placed her in the yard with the other four. After a few days of being taken out of the nest box, she seemed to get the idea and rejoined the flock.

Then a month later, we had a hen go broody again. And despite all of our Orpingtons looking exactly alike, I'm positive it was the same girl.

She'd been in the middle of a heavy molt while the other girls had molted a couple of months earlier. From my research, I gathered that when a hen is out of sync with the flock, it can lead to problems.

I think the troubles had actually started weeks before, when our little Alpha girl began chasing this hen away from the feeder. And often hassling her out in the yard. Not pecking her or anything, but this more passive hen seemed to be intimidated enough to hide out in the coop most of the day.

When I came around to refill the feeder, shaking the feed in a plastic quart container, I got into the habit of holding back a measure of feed. If this more submissive hen came out to eat, but got chased away, I'd bring her out into the yard, and give her a little pile of feed so she could eat undisturbed.

I have to say, she got pretty spoiled, and soon expected to be singled out for this treat every time!

Anyway I was discouraged that she was apparently having a second round of broodiness so soon after the first. Despite our new "no-name" policy, John and I ended up giving her one after all: Miss Broody. Because she was spending her entire day—and it appeared, her entire *life*—in a nest box.

This went on for weeks. I knew she'd likely stopped laying because I'd often discover her on an empty nest, and our egg production was two-three eggs per day inside of four or five.

So I went back to the drill. Despite Miss Broody's objections, I would gently lift her off the nest, setting her out in the yard with the others, then sprinkle a little feed for her onto the ground.

To keep her off the nest, I'd close up the nest guard.

For about two weeks, she'd go right back into the coop and either settle onto the floor, or stand next to the nests, squawking plaintively.

One spring evening, when it was nearly dark, I discovered that she had settled onto the floor for the night—apparently too intimidated to claim her spot on the roost. I guessed she'd been sleeping on the floor for some time.

My conclusion: the other hens had decided she was an outsider.

I carefully lifted her to the roost. She seemed unsure and

shaky, and after I stepped out I heard a thump. So I peeked back in. Miss Broody had jumped back down to the floor.

I tried it again. I set her back on the roost, and amazingly, there she stayed. The next night, finding her on the floor again, I once again set her on the roost. Hesitantly, she scooted closer to the other four girls.

The following day, she was spending a few hours outside with the other four. That night, when I found her on the floor and got her onto the roost, she not only scooted a little closer, but actually nestled against the huddled-up foursome.

The day after that, she was bellying up to the feeder and eating away. And the next morning, she burst out of the pen with the other girls to peck at the scratch John tossed out.

We began watching her carefully, to make sure she didn't resume her bad habits—that she had for sure fully rejoined the flock.

But it looked like Miss Broody was back to being a real hen again!

38 * STRONG INSTINCTS

*K*eeping a positive outlook, I realized long ago, comes in handy for the homesteady lifestyle. You are bound to run into setbacks, challenges, and outright troubles, but staying on the sunny side of the street always helps.

When Miss Broody rejoined the flock, I was sure my broody-prevention strategies had worked—that we were past this whole broodiness thing.

If only.

Within three weeks, she was back to her old tricks—sitting in a nest box again, all the livelong day.

Actually, a broody hen doesn't really *sit*, she settles her whole self into the bedding, fluffs out her feathers, and sinks her head into her chest. Her eyes half closed, she will appear to be in a stupor. But if you disturb her, she'll rouse instantly, and squawk —or even hiss at you!

What's interesting though, is that as soon as you lift her, she'll go sort of limp.

As I mentioned, broody hens stop laying too. The day I

discovered Miss Broody had relapsed, I lifted her out of the nest box and set her out in the yard with the other four hens.

After a long moment, she began her normal chicken behavior, scratching the ground and wiggling into the dirt for a dust bath. She ate heartily too, and when she joined the other hens on the roost that night, I was hopeful she was finally "cured."

But no.

In the next five or six days, her broody instinct *really* settled in. Every day, John and I would close the nest boxes in the early afternoon, after the other girls had had a chance to lay. But that didn't help: Miss Broody would simply sit on the floor of the coop.

We would move her out of the coop into the caged pen, or to the yard, or into the orchard, but every chance she got she would race back into the coop.

John and I ended up having to block access to the coop in the daytime, by setting a large plastic pot or rock in front of the hen door. More than once, Miss Broody managed to push the plastic pot out of the way and sneak into the coop!

Yet the days she was denied a nesting spot, once she emerged from her broody stupor, she would join the other hens. But Miss Broody absolutely would *not* sleep on the roost.

At bedtime, several nights in a row, John and I would lift her from the floor and place her up onto the roost. One night, I tried it twice. Another night, John went five rounds moving Broody. But she would immediately jump down and settle back on the floor.

I did more research, and discovered what I call "chicken whisperers"—people who really know hens, and have lots of advice about broody ones. "Breaking" is the term for trying to get a broody hen *un*-broody, and I came across many suggestions we had already tried.

But some strategies we hadn't. One remedy is a cold-water bath. Apparently a broody hen's body temperature runs high, and bringing her temp down via cold water can help break the broodiness.

Another therapy is to put the hen into "chicken jail," as one expert called it, which involves isolating the hen in a dog kennel without any bedding. That way, the hen wouldn't have any nesting material to sit on—and certainly couldn't fool herself that there were any eggs under her!

Both of those strategies seemed problematic to John and me. The bath sounded very high-maintenance, and as for the kennel, we didn't have one, and would have to build some kind of little cage.

At this point, to be truthful, I was getting discouraged. For one thing, babysitting Miss Broody was seriously impacting not only my gardening time, but my job (writing and publishing).

Also, in the last week we'd had only a few eggs from the whole flock. I suspected a brooder's pheromones were somehow impacting the other hens' egg production. I decided that our flock's reduced egg production was certainly a much larger problem than one hen not laying!

In any event, the experience was quite a lesson for me: to discover a hen's implacable instinct. And to learn that I, the puny human, had very little influence over it.

39 * MISS BROODY AND LITTLE BRITCHES

I was a slow learner.

As spring turned to summer, one hen after another turned broody. Each and every time it happened, I kept thinking it was just a fluke: that the broody hen would soon work through the process, then *every single girl* would be DONE.

Oh, how I *wish*.

In the space of a month, three more hens went broody. We ended up calling all four broody girls "Miss Broody" because we couldn't tell them apart. The one chicken we *could* identify was the girl last in line to turn broody. John called her "Little Britches."

An American history buff, John named her after one of his favorite true-life personalities from the Old West: a diminutive female cattle rustler nicknamed "Little Britches." She was a teenager who apparently was only about four foot eight inches tall, but was full of derring-do.

(Fun fact: The real-life "Little Britches" was so (in)famous that there was a 1930s feature film made about her and her partner in crime, "Cattle Annie"!)

This particular hen really *was* too big for her britches. Although she was smaller than the others, she was feisty and bossy, and as I mentioned, she was the one who became the Alpha girl early on.

She apparently decided she was in charge of both the feeder and waterer, and would often peck at the other hens and drive them off.

You might be wondering, why didn't John and I just let the broody girls be, and work through the process, even though they weren't laying?

Well, we were okay with the (hopefully) temporary loss of eggs. But a broody hen's disinterest in food, and even water, was concerning both of us, especially now that it was midsummer. Surely going days without water, a hen could die of dehydration.

John and I, then, had no choice but to continue the drill: remove the broody hen from the nest box. Then we would park her in the orchard adjoining the chicken yard, separate from the others, and set out feed and water nearby. Then close off the orchard.

But when Little Britches went broody—and shortly afterward, two *more* hens turned broody again *the same day*—I saw the writing on the wall.

My future with these chickens would be dealing with all five hens cycling through broody periods, one after the other, in more or less a continuing cycle.

And let me tell you, broody hens are a determined bunch. One evening, when I was busy watering and mulching beds, I noticed one of the separated hens had disappeared. I had moved the two broody girls in the orchard, then I looked over, and there was only one!

For a minute, I imagined the worst—that a hawk swooped down and killed her! But I was outside the whole time and nearby; I would have seen if a raptor flew into the yard.

And I would have definitely noticed the inevitable freaking out the other hens would have done.

Anyway, I quickly checked the nest boxes. And what do you know: the hen had somehow found a tiny gap in the fence, squeezed through, and snuck back to the coop and onto a nest.

I had to pull this girl out and put her into the orchard again. I know, the hen's determination to get to a nest was so epic it was kind of funny. But now that it was the high season for food gardening, I needed to be watering, weeding, and harvesting our crops. I simply couldn't spend *all* my time moving broody hens around.

Yet too soon, the girls had created yet *another* chore for us.

WITH MORE TIME in the orchard, our girls had gotten busy under the apple trees. Buffies weren't quite the little excavators our mixed flock had been, but even in their brief periods of orchard time, the five hens were starting to do some serious damage.

Our two Honeycrisp trees once again had large, deep divots around the roots, and the hens' scratching around the Queen's Cox apple made the trunk wobbly.

John, always one to see if his homesteady projects could be improved upon, once again got creative. He devised a new fencing arrangement: a stretch of four-foot steer wire that bisected the orchard diagonally, thereby cutting off the girls' access to the three apple trees.

In the orchard space nearest the chicken pen was our large Asian pear tree, and John kept that area open to them. Thick grass grew all around the tree, perfect greens for the girls.

And we had already found that no amount of scratching or digging around that tree could hurt it in the slightest: it persisted in bearing stupendously unwelcome amounts of fruit!

In any event, we hoped that giving the girls more foraging

and digging time would be an effective distraction—keeping them so happy and occupied they wouldn't get broody!

Then a new issue cropped up...

40 * CREATIVE HENS

*T*he hens had completely stopped laying.

Our five Buffies were only sixteen months old. Yet everything I'd learned about laying hens indicated that at this stage, they should be laying regularly.

Our first flock of red hens certainly had, even after three years. Even given the vagaries of nature, I'd expect a home flock should have *at least* two years of solid, steady egg production.

But in this hot and dry July, each day when I checked the nest boxes, I would be disappointed. As the girls' laying dwindled, we had been down to one egg per day for the whole flock of five.

Then, zero eggs.

Zilch.

When it comes to factors that might impact laying, John and I reviewed the usual suspects:

*Was it the heat?

Two weeks before, our region had had a freak heat wave—a "heat dome" as the meteorologists call it—over 100 degrees for several days. Our girls had definitely not been acclimated to such extreme weather. Since then, the weather had still been unusually hot, in the 80s and 90s.

*Was one hen, or several hens molting?

For sure, we had seen loads of feathers all around our girls' pen for weeks.

*Fright?

I'd heard the hens making their alarm calls frequently the last few weeks. Maybe some predators were getting a little too close, and anxiety was impacting laying.

In this busy summer, John hasn't gotten to weed-whacking the underbrush next to the pen—which unfortunately meant there was plenty of good cover for a stalking coyote or bobcat.

Despite all these possibilities, I figured the most likely cause was broodiness.

I once again wondered if having so many broody hens in short succession meant the pheromones/broody hormones had overwhelmed the laying process of all five girls.

In other words, bad hen vibes.

Needless to say, this whole broody deal was beyond frustrating. Days on end with all the labor of hen-caring, but without the reward of fresh eggs!

YEARS AGO, before we got our first flock of red hens, we selected the site for our chicken compound as close to the garden as we could. As I said, it was adjacent to our existing orchards and woodsheds—but still a fair distance away from our main yard.

Having no other real choice where to locate the whole hen complex, John ended up building it around a huge, old, big leap maple stump.

You've heard about that stump, which was right in the middle of our caged pen—where poor Buffy used to take shelter from the bullies. And you're probably wondering, why didn't we bite the bullet and dig out the stump?

LITTLE FARM IN THE HENHOUSE

Well, that bad boy was about five feet in diameter, *way* too huge to try and remove, or dismantle, even in phases.

Plus...it was maple. A super *hard* wood. And despite various parts of the stump that were decaying, despite its elderly age, it stubbornly refused to give up the ghost.

The real problem was there was plenty of live wood in there, so the stump constantly pumped out shoots of new growth.

Even the smallest branches were too dense to trim without a giant pair of loppers. Although John and I would get in there every few months to prune back the latest multiple ten-foot branches, it was a constant battle to control that crazy stump.

It was definitely here to stay.

Sure, it wasn't ideal, to have that giant, craggy hunk of wood in the middle of everything, but like I said, it did make a great chicken jungle gym.

With all my broody hen management over the last months, I had allowed the new growth get a *little* out of control. With all the sprawling branches, it was fully-leafed out with dinner-plate sized leaves (it's called "big leaf" maple for a reason).

As a result, who knew what was going on, in, on, and around the stump.

Despite all these broody hens' shenanigans, I was still doing my regular coop cleaning, which also involved picking up the manure in the caged pen. Being the middle of summer, when hens are pooing more outside, the day came when the pen required a more thorough going over.

Worming my way behind the big stump and the new branches, I checked for any droppings I should pick up before things got too fragrant.

I looked down into a small, secluded hollow between the stump and the cage. Lo and behold, there was a cache of eggs!

Those darn hens had been laying this whole time, but not in their nest boxes. For some reason, their tiny bird brains told them to lay in this new, hidden spot!

Maybe there really was something to my bad vibes and broody hens theory.

INTERESTINGLY, this little egg-laying hideaway was the furthest spot away from the nesting boxes in the coop, where the broody hens were always sneaking. So there I was, with eight eggs that I had no choice but to throw away.

As I mentioned before, the shells of freshly laid farm eggs are covered with a kind of "bloom" or a layer of protection. This protective layer is washed away during egg processing.

That's why store eggs are far more perishable than farm eggs. Still, by my calculations, some of these eggs had been out in the heat for weeks—I couldn't imagine they would be safe to eat.

So, *darn*—all those eggs wasted. It was up me to set the girls straight. I crammed a bunch of small wood debris in their laying spot, to direct them back to the nest boxes. I figured I had solved the problem.

Are you hearing a "but"?

Well, the hens did not return to their nest boxes—all of which stayed empty the next two days.

Instead, they shimmied their way past the wood debris and found an even *more* secluded hidey-hole to lay in. I knew this because after twisting myself into a pretzel to look into the tiniest recesses behind the stump, I found four more eggs!

At this point it was dawning on me that hens were a lot more creative than anyone gave them credit for.

I complained to John, our in-house keeper of common sense, about the whole "laying eggs in weird places" problem. Naturally he had an easy solution. "Why don't you just put up a fence barrier?"

Feeling stupid, I said, "Why didn't I think of that?" Wisely, John didn't reply.

The next day, I got a bunch of poultry wire fencing and crammed it into the space, covering every inch of the hidey hole. And *ta-da*! The next day, I found two eggs. In the nest boxes.

Earlier that day, I had seen a hen from my kitchen window up on the stump, appearing to look forlornly down at the hidey hole. Then she jumped off the stump. While I felt relief that I seemed to have solved their laying issues, I was sure of one thing:

Those girls were *sure* to devise yet another way to make extra work for me!

41 * THE ECONOMICS OF FARM EGGS

When it comes to keeping a backyard flock to save money on eggs, it's a no brainer. Just spend less money on their feed.

You've got lots of options:

*Give them leftovers and other kitchen scraps

*Collect worms and bugs to bring to them

*Toss extra garden crops into their pen, like squash and apples.

If you provide plenty of these other food sources, you might even be able to simply supplement their needs with chicken feed. And if you use the inexpensive stuff, your homegrown eggs will cost next to nothing.

We weren't doing any of these. John and I basically ate everything on our plates, and our kitchen scraps went into the compost. Our earthworms, we figured, did more good in the garden than they would in the hens' tummies. Collecting bugs would only work for someone with more free time than I had.

As for tossing fruits and veggies into their pen—well, you might remember our rat problem. So we met the nutritional needs of our five girls with 100% chicken feed. At this point in our hen-keeping, the math was starting to be a problem.

All summer, our hens' egg production continued to be very irregular. The two or three eggs a day had been great—while it lasted. Then the flock seemed to settle into producing one egg a day between the five of them.

If we were lucky.

I previously mentioned the organic, whole grain-and-legume feed John and I were giving our girls—definitely a luxury item. In fact, pretty much beyond our modest budget. So why did we buy this feed instead of the inexpensive corn and soy mash food pellets I mentioned earlier in the book?

John and I would tell each other, *well, it's healthy! And organic!*

We've all heard, "you are what you eat." When you're raising food, the corollary is "you are what your animals eat." Well, John and I made a point of eating high-quality, organic food, and we wanted the same for our girls.

Anyway, when I discussed our high-priced feed earlier in the book, I was deliberately vague about the cost. Because it was sort of embarrassingly high. But now that our hens were chowing down on this feed without giving back much in the way of eggs, I figured I might as well tell you the whole truth.

The cost of the feed was a hair under $40 for a 40 lb. sack. It lasted a little over a month, about 40 days. So the hens were eating about a pound of feed between them every day. Crunching the numbers, our one little egg each day was costing us $1. Meaning, the eggs we were eating cost $12/dozen!

Now, John and I didn't have any expectations of earning money from our homestead. It was always a pleasure for both of us, to raise food for ourselves and share what we could with our friends and family. Still, on our limited income, $12/dozen eggs was a pretty *big* indulgence.

Realizing the economics of our broody little flock was a

rude awakening for me. And looking back over the summer, I realized we had had exactly *one* day without a broody hen!

As I told John about my calculations, his eyes widened. "Seriously? A dollar per egg?"

"Yep," I said. "And this has gone on long enough—we've got to do something!"

I added to myself, *or at least* try *to do something*. Maybe it was a tall order, but all I wanted was to 1) Get each broody hen integrated with the flock and 2) Laying again (not just sitting on a nest in a broody trance).

I re-researched the various solutions to "breaking" a broody hen. Yes, I'd tried them already, but I wanted to see if anything new would turn up. But the general "breaking" advice was basically the same.

*Take the hen off the nest, and close off the nest boxes. This is to encourage her to return to customary hen activities, like cratching the ground for bugs, dust-bathing, and especially eating regularly.

*Get her away from the coop. Hopefully her little bird brain will maybe forget about her nest and the imaginary eggs she's trying to hatch.

*Separate her from the rest of the flock and give her lots of treats to pique her appetite. Otherwise, any bug or food scrap you give her will very likely be stolen away by the other girls.

As I said, we'd tried them all. But there was one, apparently fail-safe solution I'd heard about, but hadn't seriously considered.

*Immersing a broody hen in cold water.

I mentioned that a broody hen's body temperature runs somewhat above normal. Every time I yarded a hen out of the nest box, it was easy to detect—the chicken would feel hot. I imagine a broody hen's increased body heat, and the way she sort of spreads herself out in the nest box, is nature's way of keeping eggs warm.

The trick to "breaking," then, is to lower the hen's temperature. Still, to me, a cold dunk seemed so drastic. Cruel even. So here we were, still stuck with our one egg/day problem.

Then on one of John's trips to the feed store, a day we had two broody hens going at the same time, he told the clerk about our problem. She asked, "Have you tried a cold water bath?"

He confessed we hadn't. But after he came home and told me what she said, I looked back at all the time I'd spent shifting hens off nests and trying to get them to eat. The whole rigmarole had become, like, my *life*.

Maybe it was drastic, but I'd hit my tipping point—time to get serious about breaking the broodies.

42 * A DUNKING WE WILL GO

I didn't know what to expect with this dunking strategy, but I dressed for the job.

I donned the goofy broad-brimmed hat I always wore to clean the coop, and on top of my sweatshirt and trusty Carhartt work pants, I shrugged into John's ancient, bright green raincoat (when I wore it, he called me the Jolly Green Giant). I shoved my feet into my muck boots and pulled on a pair of thick rubber gloves.

John was on standby if something went awry, and to record the event—although if truth be told, I only needed his moral support. We hauled a hose into the orchard adjacent to the chicken yard, as well as tub we'd kept around for woodstove kindling. I also made sure the other three hens were in their fenced yard, separate from the "breaking" operation. Then I filled the tub with cold water.

Everything was ready.

Fetching one hen out of the nest, I held her firmly, hands holding down her wings and brought her into the orchard. I bent over, and stuck her in the tub.

For a few seconds, the hen didn't react. Suddenly she voiced an unearthly squawk, struggling wildly. And before I could keep her down she jumped out of the tub.

Now I knew where the expression came from: "Madder than a wet hen."

And who knew a little five pound hen could be so strong? Still, I think she was in shock, because I was able to grab her quickly and try again. For my trouble, I got water—now containing the chicken-poo dust from the hen, and a million other pathogens—splashed on my face. I mean, my *face*!

I was extremely grossed out. And this process, forcing a little bird like this, *did* feel cruel. Money was never a big motivating factor for me, especially with our hens. Yet on this day, the $1/egg price strengthened my resolve.

Despite my best efforts, I couldn't hold her down for long. In a flash, she was out, and ran to the edge of the fence, watching me warily.

By now, my pant legs were wet, I had more water on my face, and I was *really* annoyed. So all fired up, back I went to the coop for the second broody hen and proceeded back to the orchard.

I grasped her as firmly as I could, and lowered her into the water. Now that I knew how strong little hens are, I held her down with all my might.

Can you believe it? I could *not* keep that five-pound "weakling" in the tub!

Screeching, wings-flapping, she splashed the water, dousing my face, neck, and glasses. In one second flat she jumped out, running away before I could catch her.

By now, I was thoroughly disgruntled—and feeling filthy and far too ticked off for another go at the tub. However, I had high hopes that even though this cold bath was brief, it would cure the two hens' broodiness.

But only time would tell.

. . .

IN A WORD...

Nope.

The next morning, when John went out to toss the girls their morning scratch grains, four hens came out of the pen to greet him. Maybe we'd cured one hen? Both would have been great, but...

One of the hens ended up going back into the coop. Long story longer: we still had two broodies.

Later, when I lifted each broody girl off the nest, they seemed very distressed, and struggled against me, which was a first. Apparently the only thing I'd accomplished was making our two little girls scared of me. Ultimately, I don't think the cold water bath was worth stressing out the hens—*and* irritating the heck out of me.

John and I were at a standstill.

We talked about trying to obtain a different breed of hens, which aren't so prone to broodiness as Buff Orphingtons. Still, integrating new pullets into an established flock would be very tricky. Meanwhile, all I could do was hope that the approaching fall and cooler weather would bring a break from broodies.

43 * HEN-SPEAK

One early fall evening, I was turning the compost pile while I kept an eye on the five girls, not far from me in the West. They were having a fine old time, scratching in the newly-fallen big leaf maple leaves and pecking for insect treats.

As I climbed out of the shallow compost trench, collecting my shovel and spading fork, my eyes caught something in a nearby alder tree. It moved ever so slightly...

An owl! I watched it for a moment, since they're such interesting birds. I see owls only rarely, but I frequently hear their muted calls drifting from the woods around sunset.

Stepping carefully, I went to get John, busy processing wood near the coop. "Honey," I murmured, "come see the owl!"

He followed me back to the compost area, rather awed, as I was, by this rare sighting. Then the owl shifted, and glided to another tree, a little closer to the hens.

Instantly, the girls set up a racket. John and I hurried over to reassure them. *Buck-buck-bucking* like crazy, each one had her neck stretched upward, clearly a hen's "alarm" call.

I've seen frightened hens run for cover. I've also seen them freeze in the face of danger from above, like a raptor overhead.

What was interesting about this owl hovering is that the hens didn't run for cover—they must have known they'd be safe with John and me right there. So perhaps hens do this ear-splitting *bucking* to scare off trouble before it gets any closer.

The owl eventually glided off, deep into the woods. Even after it left the vicinity, the girls kept up the alarm for nearly ten minutes. At the moment, I had an epiphany.

I remembered all the noise our first flock had made years ago, when they'd been So. Very. Loud. In that moment, I realized our red flock of hens weren't just being naturally obstreperous. They'd been making their warning calls, likely because of the big cat predators prowling nearby.

It also came to me that all the interesting sounds our girls had made over the years—hen speak, if you will—actually have a purpose and meaning.

In my experience, when you hear a cackling sort of call, especially in the morning, it's probably a hen saying, "I laid an egg!" Apparently she feels compelled to share her accomplishment—and maybe brag a bit.

A "bark" is generally made by the Alpha hen, when she's trying to tell the other hens what to do, like "I'm the boss, and get away from the feeder," or "move out of my way, pronto."

There's a softer sound, a "toot" like a little horn—sometimes the girls have done this when their jostling for space around the feeder.

One more sound I've identified is a fussy, scoldy sort of sound the hens make when they're settling on the roost for the night. Roosting time often makes for interesting behavior. For example, the least favored hen might be ostracized from the top tier of the roost, and have to settle for sitting alone on the second one.

Or the "cool girls" will all huddle up together on the roost, all comfy cozy, while there might be a lone hen who doesn't fit in, and might have to keep her distance. In any event, at bedtime, hens can be somewhat snappish, with the appropriate sound effects!

I'm sure there are many more laying hen calls to interpret—spending time around your girls will teach you their hens'-speak. Still, the unprecedented wild "screeching" I mentioned before, when I was trying to give the broodies their cold-water bath?

Well, that sound seems self-explanatory: plain ol' chicken indignation!

44 * LEAVING THE HENS

With the deepening of fall, troubles in our extended family were mounting.

Emotional abuse was seriously impacting a family very dear to us—a family that included little children. Numerous times over the last months, I'd been called upon for support and frequent visits. And now, the situation, already grave, was deteriorating more each day.

I had only returned home a couple of weeks ago on a similar mission. Still, it looked like I might be needed again, very soon —and that John's presence was needed too. I began keeping my suitcase packed at all times. I could think of little else except this beloved little family in trouble.

Late one night, after yet another fraught phone conversation, I had to make a difficult decision: John and I would have to leave our place—and our hens—as soon as possible. Preparing for the seven-hour journey the next morning, I glanced out my office window.

There, I saw a coyote, not five feet away from the house.

It was the closest view I'd ever had of one. The coyote was utterly silent, apparently having no intention of making the high-pitched yelps John and I had heard so many times. Still, the sight of the animal's sharp, curious little face reminded me that two years ago, almost to the day, coyotes had killed our second flock of hens.

The thought sent a cold shiver through me. Here we were, forced to leave our girls, when these wild canines were ranging very close.

I fetched John, working in his office. "Come see," I said low. "A coyote."

He caught only the merest glimpse, before the coyote vanished.

"I don't think they've ever been so close to the house," said John.

"It feels like a hard time to be away," I said, feeling torn up inside. Our dear ones came first of course, they always would, and I knew the hens would be physically safe in their cage and coop. Yet... "The poor girls—with us gone, the emotional stress of coyotes nosing around is all they need."

"It can't be helped," said John, but he didn't look happy about it either.

JOHN and I made the trip; he returned home alone, while I stayed an extra week and a half. Those days were difficult, made more challenging by the fact that the situation had not improved. Nor had it been resolved in any way.

And it actually *had* been a hard time to be away. While John was on his own, our area experienced epic rainfall—what the meteorologists call an "atmospheric river"—with unprecedented flooding in the communities fifteen miles west of us. There were days of downpours, he told me, the like of which he'd never seen.

A wild November windstorm followed on the heels of the heavy rainfall. As it often happens around here, tall hemlock and Douglas firs sitting in saturated soils, are unable to withstand the storm winds, and will just keel over.

At our place, a sizable Douglas fir fell onto our chicken coop. John phoned me to report the storm damage—happily, the coop was pretty much unscathed. Plus the hens appeared to have slept through the impact.

All I could think was, what a boon that hens sleep so deeply at night.

THE MORNING AFTER MY RETURN, John showed me the fir. Actually, *firs*. This tree had one root system but two trunks: one had fallen in an easterly direction, and the other toward the west. While he got busy processing the windfall, I entered the caged run to hang out with the girls.

Once I got the coop-cleaning out of the way, I kept a fond eye on our clutch of blonde girls, busily scratching and pecking. As I'd hoped, the cool weather seemed to have nipped their broody instincts in the bud.

I couldn't help thinking of the resilience of laying hens. In all my years of chicken-keeping, I noticed that unless our hens were actively being stalked by a predator of some kind, they would go about their little routines through thick and thin. And without getting too bent out of shape.

By and by, John moseyed over to watch the girls with me. "It sure is good to have all five hens active again," I said.

"Yeah," said John. "I don't think we've had a broody hen for way over a month."

"One less thing to fret over, for sure," I said. With family concerns filling my mind and heart, it was a relief not to worry about a broody hen making herself sick with malnutrition or dehydration. "They all seem to have good appetites these days."

"They're not laying much, though," said John. "I think three of them are molting."

I peered at the feathers scattered around the pen. "We're still in good shape, though—I think we've got several dozen stashed in the shop fridge."

John smiled, pleased. "All set for winter, then," he said, and wandered back to the wood-cutting shed.

The girls did seem just fine. Still, over the next few days, I noticed they were just slightly *off*.

Maybe it was due to my extended absences. Or it could be that the sodden ground was way too wet for a decent dust bath. Or even that the hens been more affected by the tree crashing onto their roof than John and I thought. At any rate, the whole flock was crankier than usual.

One of hens kept chasing me and pecking my legs. I'd learned hens figure out their world through their beaks, so pecking is a natural behavior. And I was pretty sure the aggravating girl was Miss Broody. She was the hen that had gotten accustomed to the special measure of feed, separate from the others. I wondered if she was nagging me to give her extra feed again.

Then one day, she jumped against my leg and vigorously flapped her wings against me. Maybe it was her way of asking why I'd been gone so much lately!

Our little alpha hen, Little Britches, was also back to snapping at the others when I came to fill the feeder. Not just at Miss Broody, but the other hens as well—which brought on those hilarious little "toot" sounds I mentioned before. It was like a bird coffee klatch, with everyone getting a wee bit elevated over who gets the cheese Danish and who gets the bear claw.

By now, seeing how enthusiastically they were eating, I wasn't too concerned about any girl going hungry—I knew the hens (most of them, anyway) were pretty scrappy, and would sneak back to the feeder when the top girl wasn't looking!

. . .

WITH WINTER ON THE WAY, I'd just learned that giving the hens a small amount of scratch grains before bed could be helpful. Digesting the grain apparently helps raise a hen's metabolism, and with the girls in an unheated coop, I wanted to ensure their wellbeing as best I could.

I was especially thankful that John and I hadn't seen any big cats around through the fall. We hadn't detected much coyote activity either, other than the one I saw outside my window. It could be that it had been so darn rainy the predators were happy to take cover in their dens. And maybe, with the coming cold weather, they would hunker down for the whole winter. At any rate, it was a relief to allow myself to let go—at least a bit—of my worries over the hens.

Especially now. The difficult family situation was escalating. I could only worry from afar, my nerves frayed as I waited for another dreadful phone call.

NOVEMBER SLID INTO DECEMBER. There were many dark, rainy days, when it seemed like dusk was falling at eleven in the morning. Still, I'd spy a flash of blond across the yard and feel a little boost. I needed some cheering up; the way things were going for our little family in crisis, we would be leaving our place over the holidays. No one had been physically injured... yet. But the emotional violence, the threats were mounting.

John and I would, quite possibly, be needed not simply for support, but for protection.

WE DIDN'T KNOW what to expect with the visit, but as we prepared to leave our place, a severe winter storm was in the forecast. John kept to his motto of being prepared: he trundled to the farmer's supply store fifteen miles away to get a backup sack of feed, and came home with a couple of new gizmos.

Keeping the girls hydrated during cold spells was always a problem. We'd replaced our small metal waterer with a five-gallon, sturdy plastic one. But it would freeze solid almost as fast as our old waterer.

We would bring a bucket of warm water from the house out every day, but that would freeze within hours too, even when we put the bucket in the coop. The hens' body heat kept their little house slightly warmer than outdoors, but not enough to ensure their water supply.

On this trip, though, John had sprung for an *electric* chicken waterer—it would keep the hens' water thawed through the snappiest cold snap. While he was at it, he bought a new feeder too.

Our current metal feeder worked by simple gravity, and invariably the feed would get hung up in the center instead of swishing down into the feeding tray. During rainy or snowy weather, the damp grains and powdered vitamins were especially prone to caking up, and freezing solid too. A lot of feed would just get stuck just above the tray where the hens couldn't reach it.

The design of this new feeder, made of lightweight plastic, meant it would twirl more freely as the hens fed, thus distributing the feed more evenly. The feeding tray also had little dividers, so multiple birds would have their own little slot of goodies.

Clearly, this new feeder was a big improvement. We were *set*.

Leaving the hens in the dead of winter felt irresponsible, yet as I finished our last minute packing, I knew we didn't have a choice.

The phone call did come. And as I predicted, we to leave home in a rush.

45 * WINTER BLUES

While we were away, our region, all the way up and down the coast, was hit by a Christmas Day blizzard like no other. All we could do from afar was check the weather...and hope, despite the frigid temperatures, that the hens would pull through.

Thankfully, over the holiday, the situation of our little family had seemed to stabilize. Given this positive turn of events, John and I were desperate to get home. Even so, we had to extend our visit an extra day. Despite salt and plowing and every other stratagem modern people employ to carry on despite the weather, the interstate was a sheet of ice.

After dark, about forty-five miles from home, as John and I trundled along the highway at a very slow pace, a huge SUV spun out a short distance in front of us. In a fraction of a second, John, with his law enforcement driving skills, was able to swerve away from the out-of-control vehicle.

Both of us were very shaken. I had never been so relieved to arrive home. The first thing John and I did, after getting out of the car, was grab our headlamps. Gasping from the cold, we waded through the snow to the coop, and nervously, I lifted the shutter.

There, we found our five girls, snoozing away. Safe and sound.

The next morning, when John and I went outside to see how they'd fared, the girls seemed fairly perky—although their combs were pale pink from the cold. It looked like the new feeder and waterer had kept them fed and hydrated through the worst of the blizzard. And thankfully, hens know when the weather calls for staying inside their coop.

The rest of our homecoming was pretty grim, though. We had power—so it could have been worse. But our water system and all the pipes were frozen solid.

John and I hoped that after warming up the house—and therefore the crawlspace—we'd get some action out of the faucets. But no. Three more frustrating days of utilizing space heaters under the house ensued—and included some spectacularly poor judgement on my part that led to busting our pumphouse freeze plug.

After a $200 visit from a local plumber, on the fifth day, John and I had running water again.

It's funny that you don't quite appreciate the basics of modern living—like working plumbing—until you don't have them anymore. Hauling water for the chickens all the way from the pumphouse—instead of a far quicker trip from the house—had been the least of our worries. But now that we had running water again and five still-healthy hens, life seemed pretty golden.

At least it sure did once I got the kitchen cleaned up, including the mound of dirty dishes that had accumulated.

Still, the way our girls had survived the cold, on their own, I felt even more positive when the frigid Northeaster moderated a bit.

But the hens didn't get the memo: apparently they decided to stay where they'd spent the worst of the weather. Inside.

WHAT HAS ALWAYS tickled me about laying hens is their hardiness—their habit of spending every waking moment outdoors, rain or shine. They'll leave their coop as soon as they wake up, around sunrise, and stay out until sunset, when it's time for bed.

Even when it's pouring rain or freezing cold, even when a January Northeaster gale is so strong it ruffles their feathers, you'll see them outside. Even if you're an outdoorsy person like me, there are some days, I'm sure, that you have to force yourself outside. For me, that's to get a quick walk, then bring a box of firewood into the house. But I'll still find the girls scratching away in their yard.

Yet this particular January, the hens' usual behavior wasn't happening.

I couldn't blame them for staying in the coop for days on end—after all, the ground was covered with a couple of feet of snow. The daytime highs were in the teens, the nighttime lows in the single-digits. One night, we hit a zero degrees...and that's Fahrenheit, folks. I know a lot of you might think zero degrees isn't a big deal, but around here, zero about as cold as it ever gets. And the hens just weren't acclimated to it.

I could understand that after being so cold at night, the girls had decided to simply sit tight in the coop. Yet as the January days passed, and the temperatures inched over twenty degrees, they seemed to have taken up residence in there, night *and* day. It didn't help that a load of snow had blown into the girls' pen just outside the coop, so they had very little roaming area that wasn't pure snow and ice.

Scratch that: it wasn't pure!

The hens did venture out for a few minutes at a time to mill around the feeder. And soon, those few square feet of bare ground was covered with wall-to wall-hen droppings. Despite my best attempt to clean up what I could, the manure had frozen solid right into the ice.

Ordinarily, I would cover up the frozen manure with wood chips, which I use for their bedding…but with this long freeze, we were out of chips. Plus snow had covered up the pile brush we laid out for chipping. And the brush pile itself had sort of all frozen together.

After a couple of weeks without their usual free-ranging, the girls were starting to look pretty miserable. They actually sounded a bit "hen-depressed" as well. Instead of their normal squawking and scoldy talk, they would make only a few little forlorn chicken noises.

Adding insult to injury: our new feeder fell apart. I found the hens one day standing right in the feed tray. It apparently had twirled so efficiently that the screw mechanism holding it together would spontaneously *unscrew*, then the whole gizmo would fall on the ground. You'd have to sift through the grungy dirt in the run to find the various parts.

John put the feeder back together numerous times, tried a new screw, and a new washer, but nope. Finally, he threw up his hands in frustration. And even though the hens seemed to like standing in their food, he brought back the old metal feeder.

Then a few days later, the heated pet bowl failed too—John guessed it shorted out when water got into where it was plugged into the outdoor extension cord. We tried a different extension cord, and John fiddled with the wiring to the best of his ability, but nothing doing.

We'd wasted our money: ending up with just a very expensive cheap plastic bowl.

. . .

So we thought we were thoroughly prepared for winter weather...but we clearly were not.

Interestingly enough, despite their yucky environment, the girls continued to lay eggs steadily during the worst of the freeze, between the five of them, they produced a couple of eggs every other day.

Finally, the winter freeze eased up—at least enough to melt a bit of the snow. Now the girls had a small patch of exposed ground to scratch in. The semi-thaw also uncovered a bunch of sawdust sitting under John's chopsaw.

One afternoon, I gathered up as much sawdust as I could, and got it spread around on top of the manure-laden soil in the pen.

If hens could plan ahead, they'd probably be chomping on the bit to get out of the muck, and back to scratching around the orchard. I personally was making big plans to do a wall-to-wall coop-cleaning, once the manure under their roost thawed!

John, I and our girls had somehow resumed a workable winter hen routine. But by late January, I was back on the road again for our little family.

46 * DISAPPEARING HENS

*Y*et this time, I was filled with gratitude. I was away for simply a visit.

Life for our dear ones who had needed us so badly was back on an even keel, the emergency situation in the rearview mirror. I was delighted to simply be a supportive presence as the family adjusted to their new normal. Since neither John nor I were up for leaving our place—and the hens—alone once again, he stayed home to look after things.

I was away for more than two weeks. Upon my return I wanted to see the girls right away, so John and I moseyed straight over to the coop.

In winter, with the limited scratching area, the girls generally foraged pretty close together. But on this day, I saw only three chickens. Only three vibrant blond girls. Looking downcast, John cleared his throat. "While you were gone…I'm sorry to say we lost a couple of hens."

My heart sank. "When…how…?"

"I wish I knew," said John. "It was broad daylight, and they were just scratching around the orchard. But when I put them away for the night, one was missing."

Not again, I thought, feeling sick. "Oh, John…"

"A couple of days later," he said somberly, "the same thing happened—another hen was gone. I was outside all afternoon, and I never even heard them squawking."

The orchard is in plain view of the house. And as I mentioned before, when hens sense a threat, the entire flock will *buck-buck-buck* like crazy. Yet John hadn't heard anything untoward. It must have been a crafty predator to carry off a hen without her screeching.

From the small amount of evidence—a couple of patches of blond feathers on the ground, a sprinkling of more feathers close by—he and I could only guess at what might have nabbed the two girls. A hawk or owl? Both raptors are a common sight around here, and could easily have swooped down and killed a chicken instantly.

But the hawk that had gotten one of the chickens from our first flock hadn't picked up the smaller bird and taken flight—it had started eating its kill right away.

Yet what was particularly strange about losing these two girls was that the remaining Buffies didn't show any signs of trauma. After the hawk attack years ago, the other hens hid in the coop for days on end, and were nervous and jumpy long after.

But maybe these three girls never even saw their "sisters" being attacked. It could have been that a hen was dust-bathing over in a far corner while the remaining hens were picking at the feeder in the caged pen. Or that one hen had been lingering out in the orchard on her own after the others had turned in early.

I was at least relieved John hadn't had to deal with the added distress of burying maimed, dead hens. He'd done that already—too many times.

One thing I have definitely noticed over the years was that the most dramatic wildlife incursions at our place have happened when we were spending most of our time indoors. I suppose wild animals are braver about venturing out of the woods when they sense the lack of human scent and presence. Even if only one of us had been away this time, it could be that one person out in the yard doesn't deter wild critters as effectively as two would.

All this thinky-thinking aside, John and I had both been through too much heartbreak with our family situation. If a predator was coming around, I was certainly grateful we'd lost only the two hens. Given the vulnerability of chickens in the Foothills, it definitely could have been worse. And yet...

Five hens was perfect number for a bustling little homestead flock. Our Buffies were good-natured and had gotten along well; they were the cleanest flock we'd ever had too. Our five blonde girls also proven to be far more resilient than we'd hoped, making it through some very severe winter weather like champs.

REDUCED TO THREE HENS, John and I drastically changed our chicken routine. We were afraid to let them out, even into their small yard. So for the present, we would keep the girls penned up in their cage all day—a decision they weren't keen on! The Buffie trio seemed to spend a fair share of time gazing at the house, maybe puzzled why their humans weren't letting them out into the fresh air.

All the same, it wasn't easy, being philosophical about losing our chickens. For several days, I kept watching our flock, hoping one of our missing girls would reappear—like she'd only gotten lost in the woods and finally had found her way home. But for all my positive thinking, and even pretending, I knew in my heart both hens were gone.

And our little flock of three felt quite forlorn.

. . .

A WEEK LATER, Gretchen and Alan, our closest neighbors and fellow hen-keepers, lost two of their chickens, despite having a very secure pen. The evidence was similar to what we'd found our place—only patches of feathers left behind, but no entrails or animal scat. After they discovered a trail of feathers leading into the woods, our neighbors guessed it was coyotes rather than raptors.

And guessing was all we could do. The culprits remained a mystery.

47 * ANOTHER LOSS

Unbelievably, Nature struck again.

About a month later, it was getting close to sunset—the girls were getting in their last minutes of scratching around, and in minutes, they would be heading into the coop for the night. John and I had been in and out all afternoon, and figured they'd be just fine in their small pen right next to the caged safety zone.

Ready to head outside and say goodnight to the girls before they turned in, and top up the feeder, I gazed out the dining room window at the hen yard.

I noticed something strange: instead of the usual dark ground near their door, there was light material scattered all around.

Then I saw movement in the middle of the light stuff. An animal.

The light stuff was…feathers.

"John!" I cried out. "Something's got the hens!" They'd been attacked. Right in front of my horrified eyes.

I started to cry as John ran to the back door and shoved his feet into his shoes. A small coyote? Then the animal moved its head. I saw it was a red-tailed hawk.

I yanked on a sweatshirt as John raced outside. The hawk must've heard a human coming, because it flew off. I caught up with John next to the fence. He said, "She's still moving."

"Get some gloves on, honey." A sob caught in my throat as I entered the chicken yard. I found a hen, lying on the ground—a big bloody gash at the top of her breast. And completely still.

Still weeping, it was an effort to call to John. "She's not moving now—you must've just seen her in her death throes."

As he went back to the shop for a coat, I frantically gazed around the yard. So where were the other two girls?

I hoped against hope they had gotten into the coop in time. I went inside and saw only one hen. She was milling around, not on the roost. "You're *okay*, I said softly. Still, I was only a little relieved.

I went back into the yard and looked around. Some twenty feet away from the dead chicken, in the corner next to one of the woodsheds, I saw a patch of blond and ran to it.

It was a hen. She'd wedged herself into the corner so tightly she was halfway under the slats of the shed. She wasn't moving. Yet there was no blood. Or feathers on the ground.

But I was afraid she was dead too—from fright. I stroked her back. "Are you alive, little girl?"

The hen moved ever so slightly. "Let me pull you out," I told her, and gently put my hands on either side of her and drew her toward me. She resisted, and only burrowed further under the slats.

The fact she'd been strong enough to resist made me hope she was uninjured. I hurried out of the pen and around to the front of the shed, to see if I could pull her out. Boxes of small logs and wood scraps were piled in the corner where the hen was hiding.

I pulled the boxes away—and there she was, whole. She blinked.

"You *are* alive," I said, still a little weepy, just John approached.

"She's okay?"

"Yes—but maybe she'll want the "rooster" to help her," I said through my tears.

The hens have always been more compliant with John. Sure enough, he was able to lift the unresisting hen. He and I returned to the coop, and he gently placed her inside.

Two live hens. It was something to be grateful for.

But we still had to face the dead hen. As John and I approached the body, I took a long hard look. I'd seen worse, when the cougar had gotten our first flock and left pieces of the chickens all over the cage. But still, I started crying again. "I'm sorry honey, this is my fault."

"No it's not," said John. "It's just nature. And remember, we just lost two hens on my watch."

True, John had been the one looking after our place while I was away. But this—the hen getting killed—really did feel like my fault: I'd let them out of their cage just a half hour ago. When the hawk attacked, I was just minutes from going out to the pen.

"We'll bury her where I buried the other hen," John said. I knew he meant the hen from our first flock years ago, that had also been killed by a hawk. He lifted the dead hen. Her head dangled. "Her spine's been completely broken."

"I'll...dig the hole," I said with difficulty. I hadn't wept years ago, while I cleaned up pieces of Dottie and the other red hens. But now, I couldn't seem to stop crying. I grabbed a small shovel and followed John to a stump a little ways from my compost piles. He cleared away a bit of brush.

Furious with myself, I savagely sank the shovel into the ground.

Losing this hen felt so different from the other two the previous month. Then, there had been no bodies. And I'd been away caregiving, my mind full of worries and the family troubles I was facing. Now, actually seeing the hen getting killed hit me in a whole new way.

Not that burying her helped. I dug a small hole about a foot deep, and John nestled the hen in it. He covered her up, filling the hole and patting the earth as he finished. "You're safe in hen heaven now," he told her.

"Away in the Happy Hunting Ground." I swallowed past the lump in my throat and trudged back to the coop.

I went to say hello to the other two hens—they were still awake—and filled the feeder. One of them actually came out to the feeder and nibbled a little. Then as they climbed on the roost, I returned to the yard and tried to clean up the feathers, raking them into two piles. But there were still so many more scattered around.

A cold northeaster was forecast for early the next day. I hoped the gale would blow the feathers away. To help take my mind off the killing.

I knew John's heart was as heavy as mine. Before he went in, I said, "Now that the hawk knows it's found a reliable food source, it's going to keep coming back here until it gets every last hen." He nodded soberly.

We both knew the hen-caring policy we'd started a few weeks ago had been *wrong*.

We'd always wanted to let our hens out of their wire-covered cage every day, to scratch and nibble on weeds, get a little sunshine—or on a cloudy day, simply get some natural light.

But going forward, we couldn't let the hens out of their cage into their uncovered yard just because we were home, and could see them through the window. Nor could we let the hens out while we were outside, doing garden chores or chopping firewood nearby.

After learning yet again of the relentlessness of wild predators, John and I had to institute a whole new rule: we absolutely could *not* let them out of their cage unless we were right there in the yard with them.

The hawk attack had come without warning—the big raptor hadn't first made an exploratory pass over the yard or anything. Just boom!—attack. John and I couldn't trust this bird, or its compadres, not to try again. Hawks are such majestic creatures, but with this attack, I hated them.

It was a hard lesson. And now our little flock of Buffies was down to two.

48 * HENS DON'T FORGET

Nearly two weeks had passed since the hawk attack—and our two remaining girls were still traumatized.

It had taken me a day or two to realize it, but our favorite hen, feisty Little Britches, had been spared. Maybe she had eluded all the predators in the last months because she was smarter and quicker than the others. Yet the fact that this particular girl survived was something to be grateful for.

But for all her feistiness, Little Britches seemed to have lost her courage; the hawk attack had been as hard on her as the other hen. For the first five days afterward, the two of them wouldn't leave the coop—not for food, not for water. It appeared they were spending their days just milling around the coop floor, or hanging out on the platform under their roost.

I would open the people door and say, "It's okay, you're safe." I tried coaxing them out with feed or scratch, but they wouldn't budge. All I could do was sprinkle some feed on the wood chips on the floor, which they would peck at only halfheartedly. I put a bucket of water in the coop too, since they wouldn't come outside to drink from their waterer.

Their eating pattern had changed too: usually, fresh feed in the feeder would have them eating with gusto. Now, just like the other hen, even our brave Little Britches only pecked at the bits, once, twice—then she would stop eating, lifting her head to check her surroundings. Over and over.

Finally, the day came when they emerged from the coop of their own accord.

But they only stayed outside for a couple of minutes. The next day, they came out a couple of times—yet again, would only stay for a brief time. The two of them hardly ate anything; they were too busy doing their new "peck-peck-look around" habit to take in much nourishment. Then they would disappear back into the coop.

Yet another sign showed that our hen twosome was still distressed. They had been excellent layers before the hen was killed, but after the attack, they stopped laying entirely.

Years ago, after our first-ever loss of a hen to a hawk, the five other girls had also hunkered down in the coop. But they had stayed there for only three or four days. These two Buffies were clearly far more traumatized.

But why?

Buff Orpingtons are known to be gentler than most laying breeds, and I wondered if they were simply less resilient. And if hens generally sensed there was more safety in numbers, maybe with only the two of them, Little Britches and the other hen felt more vulnerable.

It also occurred to me that since our Buffies have been so prone to broodiness, maybe these two were far more comfortable spending days on end inside their coop than our other hens had been.

But it was sad to see them decline. Especially Little Britches, who had always been so energetic. With so little exposure to sunlight, the girls' combs were turning paler. And they seemed to have lost their zest. I actually *wanted* the girls to peck at my legs again, telling me, "C'mon, I want some special treats!"

With the constant pressure from predators around here, sometimes I felt we were in a losing battle. Alan and Gretchen had lost a third hen just before the hawk attack at our place. Their flock, like ours, was shrinking: they were down to only three chickens.

Our friends, *and* John and I, came to the same conclusion. The only way to get our hens back to free-ranging again was to go all out on protection: completely cover the entire chicken yard with netting or steer wire.

For us, it would be a big job: our hen yard is at least 15'x15'. We would need new supports going down the middle, and the way hens scratch, making huge divots in the ground, it would take a *lot* of muscle to bury the posts deep enough. So for now—at least until our two girls were interested in venturing back into the sunshine—their caged pen would have to do.

With this latest development, John and I immediately changed our egg consumption. Gone were the days of three-egg omelets, or other egg-forward recipes. Before the girls stopped laying, we had built up a little stash—a couple of dozen eggs. But now that we had zero expectation of more, John and I would ration those precious 24 eggs. He and I knew it wouldn't be long before we had to buy store eggs again.

But whatever adjustments we needed to make to our eating *or* our homestead, I just wanted our girls to feel *safe*—have a normal, henny life again.

THE DAYS PASSED. I was starting to think the two girls would stay in their coop forever.

They still weren't laying. What really had me concerned, however, was that they stopped *acting* like hens. Like they were fading away right before my eyes.

I was afraid they would eventually succumb to starvation.

Little Britches had always been more cunning about getting

more food than the others. It was doubly hard to see her only pecking listlessly at the feeder once or twice a day. It certainly wasn't enough food to keep either hen alive for the long run. And what was particularly heart-wrenching was that both girls *knew* where the hawk had killed their "sister."

They wouldn't step foot near the side of the pen closest to the yard. And both girls would certainly not venture anywhere *near* the pen door, which was only a few feet from where the other hen had died. Even when John and I visited their pen, to coax them out into the world again, the girls just weren't interested.

But we persisted. And finally one day, accompanied by John and me, the two hens very slowly ventured into their yard.

They nibbled at a few blades of grass. Yet I saw with distress that their new eating habits had become ingrained: one, two pecks, then they would lift their heads to scope out their surroundings. Clearly, the girls still didn't feel safe. I wondered if they would ever again eat and explore the way they used to. As for laying again—well, that seemed like a distant dream.

But our egg supply was the least of our problems. Even after all this time, the girls still weren't engaging in normal hen behavior: taking dust baths or scratching. One day I decided to mix things up a little—shake the girls out of their funk.

Next to their yard was a narrow area between the outside of their fence and one of our woodsheds. It's always chock full of weeds and thick clumps of grass. I hoped that in such a confined space, they could let down their guard. And if that juicy green grass didn't get them scratching, nothing would.

So John and I herded them into this small rectangle, closed them in with a length of steer wire, and hovered over the space. The girls did seem to like the grass, and gave it a few semi-enthusiastic pecks. Then they wanted OUT.

"Girls, give it a chance," I coaxed them. "Stay just a few more minutes?"

But the two hens were *not* having it. Even with John and me right there with them, they continued to pace the short length of wire, making distressed sounds. I didn't want them to get re-traumatized, so we let them out—and they made a beeline for the coop.

"I guess our experiment failed," I glumly said to John.

Or had it?

Gradually, the girls began spending more time outside the coop. When I came into the pen to feed them, I could tell they'd been eating more. Then one day, I saw an encouraging sign they might return to their normal, energetic routine: I found little round depressions in the loose dirt in one corner of their caged pen—they'd been dust-bathing...

Which meant, easing back into instinctive behavior!

I've mentioned dust-bathing before, an instinctive behavior of laying hens. They will scratch out a shallow hole, and sink right into it, fluffing the dirt around them with their wings. The goal is to get soil and dust in and among their feathers, which apparently discourages parasites. They'll do this as much as several times a day.

Three days after our experiment, when I came to see them, the hens ventured into their yard without too much coaxing. They pecked at some grass, and actually started to scratch a little. I couldn't believe it—the girls were *finally* back on track!

Then...a large bird flew over our place.

They looked skyward immediately, then the large bird *cawed*. And the girls scuttled right back into the cage. "C'mon kids," I told them, "it's only a raven, you're okay. It wasn't even that close!"

But they were done being outside for the day.

Still, both girls were slowly starting to spend most of the daylight hours out in their pen, and I saw more signs of dust-bathing. And their appetites were returning. While they were still doing their peck-peck, look-around thing, they were spending a lot more time at the feeder.

John and I were able to coax them out into the yard again, and with us chaperoning, they pecked at the dirt. They scratched a little too. And before long, their scratching was back to the serious stuff: strong, deep scratching, claws tearing at the weeds with a *scritchy* sound.

And *finally*, low and behold, three weeks and a day since the attack, I found an egg in one of the nests!

After that first egg, the girls seemed eager to get out in their yard again. They were scratching with gusto too, and even climbing up on the old maple stump—all happy hen activities. And judging from all the droppings in their pen, they eating normally again. Maybe making up for lost time.

What was clear was that the hens could never go back to free-ranging all day, to get the light and bugs and scratching time they needed. Still, for me, this experience was a useful lesson in hen-keeping. Our girls, it seemed, needed to recover in their own good time. Not according to humans' timeframe or expectations.

It's how nature works, I suppose. Healing happens when the time is right...and not before.

49 * A NEW THREAT

When it comes to wildlife invasions at our place, I thought I'd seen it all.

But on a lovely spring day, the hens started making some weird sounds—not their usual *buck-buck- bucking* alarm call, but one I hadn't heard before: strange, high-pitched shrieking.

I jumped to the window to see a hen *flying* off the big maple stump, still screeching—and a large, dark shape hovering over the girls' caged pen: good-sized critter had climbed up the steer wire fence and was terrorizing the girls from only a few feet away.

ON TOP of the cage!

I ran outside and the dark shape immediately slunked into the woods—but as it jumped over our fence about forty feet away, I saw the black streak on its tail. A coyote.

At least the girls were physically safe in their caged pen. As their voices changed to their *buck-buck* alarm call, I called out to them, over and over, "It's okay, it's gone, you're safe."

As the two hens gradually settled down, I returned to the house, sighing, and changed into my work gear. I thought I'd better go into the pen and spend time with the hens for reassurance. After such a dramatic encounter with a killer—I mean, the climb on top of the cage was a first—I was afraid we would be in for a lather-rinse-repeat: that the girls would retreat back to the coop, lose interest in eating, and stop laying for a long while.

I was wrong. Even though they were newly healed from their hawk trauma, these two girls proved to be more resilient about the critter climbing on top of their cage. They didn't run straight into coop, just sort of loitered around the pen, and after a little while, pecked at their feeder. And when I refilled it, they ate heartily.

The next morning, they were out as usual, roosting on the big stump. And the biggest surprise: two eggs in the nest! And as the days passed, they continued to lay, better than ever.

The thing is, for months, since we lost first the two hens, then a third to the hawk, I'd been sort of pretending to myself: that keeping the girls locked up in their caged pen all day was only temporary. That one day soon, we could let them back in the orchard, to live a hen's dream life in the sunshine, pecking at bugs and weeds all the livelong day.

But now that I knew for sure the coyote(s) weren't giving up, I *really* had to get real. Our girls would have to live out their days in the cage. It's true, this completely secure space was pretty large for hens' digs. At about 20' x 10', the cage provided our two Buffies had more room than they could possibly know what to do with.

Plus the big-leaf maple stump at one end served as a hen jungle-gym of sorts, and a favorite roosting spot. And all spring and summer, I could toss a bunch of freshly pulled weeds in the pen for them to scratch in.

Yet with all these amenities for the girls, I still felt…discouraged. With predators from the ground *and* from the sky, John and I knew *relentless* didn't fully describe just how severe the predator situation was at our place.

Especially one day a couple of weeks later. I was just leaving for a bike ride when I heard the girls' alarm call again. I jumped off my bike and hurried to their cage.

Little Britches was looking very vigilant, neck stiff, peering around, and the other hen had disappeared inside the coop. Maybe the coyote had paid another call—but our brave Little Britches must've known she was safe. And when I returned from my ride, the other girl had come back out, both of them milling around as usual. Who knows. Maybe they were actually getting used to being hassled.

I couldn't get used to it though. Later that afternoon, I did let them out into their fenced yard while I did some weeding just a few feet away. They seemed to enjoy scratching in the new spring grass, but it was absolutely nerve-wracking seeing them out in the open, even as close as I was. A hawk could descend on a hen in seconds, a coyote climb a fence and snatch one just as quickly. I breathed a sigh of relief when they went inside for the night.

THE NEXT DAY, I got the wake-up call.

I was heading for the coop, skirting past one of our woodsheds when I heard a *thump*…then a rustle. And just feet away, a large, tawny shape leaped through the shed and streaked away. A bobcat! It was clearly stalking our hens again.

It was the tail that had fooled me—made me believe our predator had been a coyote. I hadn't seen a bobcat for a year or so and had forgotten that a bobcat's tail is simply shorter than a house cat's, not completely bobbed. And this creature had a black streak on its tail.

Everything became clear: It was a bobcat's tail I had seen as it jumped our fence a few weeks back, a bobcat that had been hassling our girls this week. And the odds were excellent that it had been a bobcat systematically killing our neighbor's chickens.

And now that we had seen, close-up, how menacing bobcats could be, I could put my climbing coyote theory to rest—it had simply been my imagination going into overdrive.

In any event, the culprit didn't matter: coyote or bobcat, they still wanted to eat our hens. Nature, I was forced to admit, is not just relentless, but inexorable. As much as we humans think we can control or outsmart the weather or wildlife, nature will win every time.

Yet since the hawk attack, I observed a new development with the hens. It was interesting and at the same time, sad: the girls bedtime routine changed. Hens have sort of a light sensor in their brain structure—a gland—which cues them when the daylight starts to dim prior to sunset. And it's this light sensor that tells the hens to go into their coop for the night.

The hawk attack happened a little while before this change in daylight. And ever since that early evening, our two girls began turning in significantly earlier than they used to: almost an hour before sundown. And although they had returned to their other normal hen behaviors, I'm guessing that terrible incident was imprinted on their brains for the long term.

Like I said—hens don't forget.

50 * BROODY AND ANXIOUS

Mid-spring rolled around—and with it, our first warm spell.

John and I were still keeping the girls in their caged pen all day, but springtime had its rewards: we tossed rich green leafy weeds to the girls, and judging from a hapless moth that both hens chased to its death, a few sure-to-be tasty bugs were venturing into the cage too.

Unfortunately, the warmer temperatures brought something else as well: the apparently inescapable Buffie broodiness.

One sunny late April day, I went to make my regular hen rounds, and found a hen on the nest. Now, if she was laying, she was doing her job. But this girl was still on the nest at three in the afternoon. All I could think was, *Not this again!*

I realized this particular hen, who along with Little Britches had survived all the other predators, was the most determinedly broody of the entire flock. Miss Broody—it was our generic name for whatever hen is broody, and now that we were down to two hens, that would be her moniker forever more—was worthy of her name.

As the days passed, she was hunkered on a nest 24/7, and no

amount of coaxing would get her off. As I had done the summer before, I lifted the outside nest box cover to extract a very ornery hen off the nest, take the long way around to the caged pen, and place her in front of the waterer. And hope she would take a drink.

If Miss Broody turned up her nose at water, she was even less interested in food. She would take a peck or two of feed, then just as before, run back to the coop as soon as she could. It was up to me, then, to force the issue: get her to eat and drink enough to stay alive.

Once I got her off the nest and into the pen, also like the previous summer, it was time to block the hen door. This small act—for her benefit, mind you—soon became a battle of wills. Would the human prevail? Or the hen?

I started off shoving big rock into the hen door. But to completely block the opening, I needed such a big stone that lifting it off the ground was a bit of a strain on my back. I explored the yard near the coop to see if I could find something more convenient.

One day, I stuffed a small cardboard box into the hen-sized opening. When I returned to the compound, it had been pushed aside, and Miss Broody was back on her nest. Another time, I shoved the bottom of a plastic planter into the opening. When I returned to the compound, the planter was askew. Sure enough, there she was, on the nest again.

I don't know how she did it, but Miss Broody was one resourceful hen!

Okay, stronger measures were called for. The next day I not only shoved that planter in the little door opening, but lodged it in tightly. *That*, she couldn't move. Yet she made her displeasure clear, pacing back and forth in front of the blocked hen door, squawking in protest. I could tell she wasn't going to eat or drink anything more, and was just using up hen energy.

I finally relented and removed the pot—which meant we were back to square one.

Through Miss Broody's current "confinement" (the old-fashioned word for pregnancy), Little Britches had been staying in the coop all day. In the past, I would have immediately guessed that she was broody as well—after all, over the last year and a half we'd often had two Broodies at the same time. But with my frequent coop-checking, I knew she wasn't on the nest.

Just milling around inside the coop.

I wondered if she was a bit lonesome. Now that we only had the two girls, Little Britches had no one to pal around with. Maybe she was just enjoying hanging out inside with her "sis." Still, every time I came out to refill the feeder, Little Britches would emerge to greet me, but wasn't quite herself. She was normally a good eater—like I said before, she had a talent for worming her way around the others to get the choicest bits of feed. But this particular week, she only half-heartedly picked at the feeder.

She wasn't sick or anything, since she was still laying. But one day, I watched her at the waterer…and her behavior told the full story. She would take a quick drink, then stop, stretch up her neck, and look around, before taking another sip. It was exactly the same behavior both girls exhibited after the hawk attack in early spring.

I concluded the bobcat had been sniffing around again.

It had only been three weeks since I'd found the bobcat on top of the cage, menacing the girls. If the cat was back, no wonder she was anxious, and had retreated into the coop.

Playing it safe inside, Little Britches was also up to a hen's customary scratching on the coop's dirt floor. Instead of the previously packed-down floor covered with wood chips, she'd created piles here, divots there, and nice little hollow for dust-bathing.

It was truly amazing, how one small bird could move around such large quantities of dirt. I could only hope that the bobcat—denied a chicken dinner—would eventually give up, move on, and go chase rabbits like it was supposed to.

In the meantime, I decided it wouldn't really hurt Little Britches to loiter in the coop another week or two.

51 * A TERRIBLE MYSTERY

A few days later, I made my usual visit to the chicken compound. Passing the caged pen, I saw no sign of Little Britches. She was obviously hanging out with Miss Broody in the coop, so I opened the man door to lure her out with some feed.

Sighing at the state of the floor—there were even more dirt piles than the day before—I looked around. There was no other hen in the coop. Only Broody, sitting placidly in the nest box.

I stepped out of the coop and glanced hurriedly around the caged pen. No hen. I looked behind the big maple stump, to see if Little Britches was poking around in the decomposing wood at the base. But nothing.

Miss Broody, sitting on the nest, was the only hen in the compound. Little Britches was *gone*.

Sick at heart, I raced to the house and called to John, "The bobcat got another hen!"

Hurrying back to the coop with John, I couldn't believe what was happening. How could this be? I had locked both girls into the cage last night. And there was no sign of an intrusion. The caged pen's only openings, if you could call them that, was the

2" x4" steer wire it was made of. There were no feathers strewn around indicating a struggle, no clutch of feathers adjacent to the fence, where the cat might have tried to pull her out.

No blood anywhere.

Clearly, the bobcat had returned, and carried Little Britches away.

But how?

52 * OUT OF OPTIONS

John and I swiftly searched the compound's perimeter. In the orchard next to the chicken yard was a swathe of gold feathers. We really had lost Little Britches.

Four of our five hens killed since January. Our little flock, decimated.

My heart like lead, we returned to the caged pen. Before we brought home our second mixed flock, he had rebuilt the pen/cage as snugly and securely as it could possibly get. Double poultry wire around the bottom two feet of the cage, each and every tiny gap between the fence and building was reinforced, and the same for the fence around the maple stump. Steer wire covered the enclosure, firmly stapled to the fence frame.

There was no way the bobcat could have gotten into the cage. But he'd killed our girl nevertheless. For the life of us, we could not see any *way* Little Britches could have escaped from the steer wire enclosure either.

I was haunted by an image of our terrified little hen running frantically around the cage while the bobcat menaced her from above, crawling on top of the steer wire. Going around the cage

I checked the wire on one corner at the top of the cage, not far from the feathers.

The wire was slightly loose.

I wondered if our poor girl Little Britches had flown wildly around until she hit that loose corner. And being smaller and quicker than the other hens, that she had *somehow* managed to slip through.

Escaping from the bobcat to what she *thought* was safety. Instead, all signs pointed to the bobcat simply leaping over and seizing her just a few feet outside the cage.

WITH THIS LATEST LOSS, I realized that what we *thought* was a secure chicken area wasn't safe enough.

As the old saying goes, "hindsight is 20-20." John and I had used ½" hardware cloth in the garden to line the bottom of our raised vegetable beds—the one failsafe material to keep voles out. Now, I knew that John and I should have built the entire compound using hardware cloth. Bolted down. It would have created a barrier no animal could squeeze through, and no hen could escape from. If we truly wanted a predator-proof compound, we should have electrified the surrounding fencing too.

And speaking of predators—you might wonder, why hadn't John and I decided to hunt down the bobcat, after the last time it got a hen? Solved the problem?

But this bobcat was just doing what bobcats and every other creature does. Eating to survive. John and I both felt strongly that to kill the larger carnivores—the apex predators as they're known—upsets the whole wildlife balance. And without bobcats, coyotes and mountain lions, what mechanism would keep deer, rabbit and rodent populations down?

As for the many changes in our neighborhood, they weren't the bobcat's fault either. Our immediate area had seen numerous clearcuts the last few years—hundreds of acres of forested land cut down. Other woodlands nearby have been cleared for development—all that wildlife habitat reduced. Or eliminated.

Since big cats range over many dozens of miles, it makes sense that they would move from those cleared tracts toward uninhabited areas. Our property includes about eight and a half acres of untouched woodlands. Since we also have bears in the neighborhood—we find new scat nearly every day on our lane from spring till fall—John and I generally don't go into our woods. Our acreage also has forest tracts on two sides, where there is no human activity either.

It was likely that a bobcat, or more than one, had settled near our place, in these quasi-wild areas. Especially with a reliable food source at the ready: chickens.

Now that we only had one hen, what was our next move? With our goal of food self-reliance, it made sense to John and me to replenish our flock.

Yet, we hesitated. Our hens' cage, which we were so sure was completely safe, turned out not to be. What more could we have done? What more could we do?

Part of me wondered: was it wrong to bring more hens to our place?

53 * A LONE AND LONESOME HEN

As John and I adjusted to losing Little Britches, and to our one-hen homestead, Miss Broody was adjusting too. By apparently taking up permanent residence inside the coop.

This hen had always marched to a different chicken drummer than the rest of our Buffie flock. Most notably, she was the champion broody hen in a flock geared for broodiness.

The year before, her first broody session was typical. Generally, broody hens will go about 21 days, the time it takes to hatch eggs. But as the months went by and Miss Broody cycled in and out of more broody periods, each session lasted longer and longer. And the stretch of time when she was actually eating regularly and laying grew shorter.

I'd always wondered if her broodiness stemmed from being the low hen in the flock's pecking order. Not an enviable spot in the hen world; as I mentioned, the others had bullied her from time to time. By day, they wouldn't always let her get to the feeder, and at night, they often wouldn't make room for her on the roost.

But she was scrappy in her own way. And possibly smarter

than I guessed. As I said before, when the other hens would push her away from the feeder, she learned to chase me around until I gave her a special measure of feed. And when the flock made their danger call, she was always the first one to run into the coop to lay low until the danger was over.

A little animal story: my younger sister, the one who grieved so long for our dog Snoopy in my childhood, is a horse girl. She's owned and cared for four horses most of her adult life, and through thick and thin, has been deeply connected to them emotionally. Now, the remaining two are growing elderly.

Recently, she was taking care of her 25 year-old mare Honey, a gentle, well-mannered animal, and wondering aloud if her horse was nearing the end of her life. Honey promptly kicked her in the leg!

My sister limped for quite a few days after, but learned a big lesson: don't talk about that kind of stuff in front of your animal. So like horses and other domesticated critters, it could be that Miss Broody was more intelligent and more intuitive than John and I ever thought.

And maybe her scrappiness was the reason she was the lone survivor of three bobcat raids and one hawk attack. But it sure didn't keep her from being broody.

THIS PAST SPRING, Miss Broody had been the first of our flock of three (at the time) to go broody; on the first warm spring day, she retreated to the coop. Around the three-week mark—about the timeframe we would expect the broody stage to be over—she got a shock.

It was when her only remaining chicken chum, Little Britches was killed. I think at that point, Miss Broody apparently entered a new phase of chicken-ness.

She holed up in the coop and there she stayed.

Each and every day, I would haul her off the nest and try to coax her to take some nourishment—put some feed right under her nose, then carry her to the waterer. *Then* I would stand next to her until she took a sip. Her drink lasted only a few seconds before she'd run straight back inside the coop.

She had gone through long periods of broodiness before, so long that I thought she'd just wither away. Yet here she was, still surviving. But she'd never been broody *this* long.

Certain that the bobcat was an ongoing threat, I figured she and I needed a new routine, to keep her going for the long run. I started putting her out in the grass and locking her out of the pen. For a little while, I would simply stand over her, and keep her company. Without access into the coop, Miss Broody would actually eat a little clover, and when I put a measure of feed on the grass, she'd peck at the whole grains.

Yet just as she had for several months, between pecks of food, she would look around fearfully. All in all, she was consuming very little food. It finally came to me what the real problem was.

She was lonesome. Maybe she even had some kind of hen depression. Still, all I could do was *make* her stay outside for those few moments.

But after a few weeks, the light and the rich spring grass finally worked its magic. On a warm June day, I looked across the yard and saw a vivid splash of blond on the big maple stump. Miss Broody was roosting outside!

After being broody for over seven weeks, she had finally left the nest of her own accord—easing back to her "henny-ness!"

A COUPLE OF WEEKS PASSED. She still wasn't laying.

I wondered if laying hens need the presence of other hens to keep their egg-producing hormones up to speed. With Miss Broody living solo, maybe she would never lay again. I could see she was still very anxious—eating or scratching, she continued to look around constantly for threats. A frightened hen is not much of a layer.

Still, I had hopes, especially one summer evening when our neighbor's cat ventured into the yard. Miss Broody began making her *buck-buck-buck-bu-GAH!* warning call, just like a "real" hen. So I kept checking the nest every day... only to be disappointed

Our nearest neighbors, Alan and Gretchen, who had sold us our flock, were also down to one hen—the bobcat had systematically decimated their chickens too. Their one hen was still laying, but Alan told us that she was eating her eggs—which is very dysfunctional chicken behavior. I guessed this hen was lonely too.

At any rate, it wasn't long before Miss Broody relapsed back to broodiness. And despite the warmth and sunshine, the rich grass, and the smorgasbord of summer bugs, she was apparently *done* with the great outdoors.

I WASN'T SURPRISED. Yet with this latest broody phase, my disappointment went deeper than simple resignation. As I mourned Miss Broody's gone-but-not-forgotten "sisters," I did a lot of thinking about our homestead. And it all came back to me:

Once you start keeping laying hens, your girls are the heart of your homestead. And now that we were down to one nervous little chicken, there was a hole in the heart of our Little Farm.

54 * DON'T STOP BELIEVIN'

*A*t this point, I pretty much gave up hope that Miss Broody would ever again be a happy, productive hen.

As the summer weeks passed, her broody habit was definitely out of control. After two-plus months of it, her comb was a pale, sickly color, a beige-pink, instead of a Buffie's normal bright red. Still, I persisted in my fruitless attempts to get her to be a hen again.

Each day, just like all the other times she'd been broody, I was back to the drill: lifting her off the nest. Despite a little indignant hissing—the only evidence of Miss Broody's life force—I would put her in front of the waterer. Then I'd stick around until she drank, and coax her into having a little feed.

It didn't last long; after a few pecks, unless I blocked the hen door, she would run back into the coop.

I was determined to do everything I could to keep her going. And if she died of malnutrition and dehydration, I would know I'd done everything I could.

AUGUST ROLLED BY. I saw the writing on the wall.

This poor little animal was eating barely enough to stay alive. She was going to live out her days alone in the coop, pale and sickly, until she simply gave up on life.

After all this, I would have been *thrilled* if she came out of her broodiness, even more so if she laid an egg. But I would have been satisfied if she simply fulfilled her hen destiny: scratching the ground, enjoying her feed, chasing bugs…and hanging out with John and me.

Yet I was most concerned about her loneliness—as I talked about before, hens are herd animals, meant to live with others. And without any other hen companionship, whether it was dust-bathing in the daytime, or roosting cozily together at night, I couldn't see any future for Miss Broody at our place— forever under the threat of a bobcat or other predators.

I hated giving up on Miss Broody. But was it finally time to try and find a new home for her?

ONE DAY, I heard Miss Broody doing some low-key chattering. Now *that* was certainly new. Usually, broody hens, sunk onto their nest, are utterly silent. Perhaps she'd sensed a predator? But when I went out to see her, she was still as broody as broody can be.

So just like I'd been doing for months, I had to yard her off her nest and get her to eat.

I hadn't completely lost hope yet, though. That evening, winding up my chores, I peeked into the coop. Miss Broody was on the *roost!*

This was *big*—a normal hen behavior. And when I rattled her feeder, she actually emerged from the coop and ate a little! And what do you know: the next day, she left the coop to come into the pen *on her own.*

And she briefly hung out on the big leaf maple stump. This was even *bigger!*

Whatever the future held for Miss Broody, she had definitely set a record for the longest broody period by far of any of our hens. And now, all signs pointed to her broodiness being on the wane.

Naturally I had to check the nest.

No eggs. To be honest, I didn't really expect any. Still, I dared to hope that with my encouragement, Miss Broody's "normal" behaviors would stick.

If they did, for more than a few days, maybe she could regain her healthy eating and hydration habits. It would likely take lots of protein and nutrients, vitamins and minerals to recapture her former vitality. Even more to produce eggs.

But what did eggs matter? Miss Broody had come back to life!

55 * MISS BROODY'S PERSONAL BEST

*I*n late summer, haze from regional wildfire smoke has become a regular feature in our area.

This season was no different—except this year, the haze was more intense and lingered for weeks, dampening my spirits. But Miss Broody's breakthrough was a joyful event.

That first day she emerged from the coop, her outdoor play time didn't last long. Yet August drew to a close, she began to spend longer periods outside. Then one day, she appeared in the run first thing in the morning—and stayed outside until sundown.

Like a normal hen!

Suddenly, she was powering down the feed, and was scratching the ground constantly, like a laying hen ought to. Our previously languishing Miss Broody had a whole new lease on life.

I let myself hope—like, *seriously* hope—she would start laying again.

. . .

EACH DAY, when I came to take care of her, she was practically pushing on the door to get out of the run and into the yard. She was pecking at clover and other greens like never before, and emptying her feeder regularly too.

Yet what was entirely new was her energy and feistiness: whenever I opened the gate to the chicken yard, this previously retiring little girl would actually try to escape into the woods.

And she was molting like crazy. As I mentioned before, molting is a normal, cyclical process: a hen loses a lot of feathers while her reproductive system takes a break. It had been many months since Miss Broody had molted, and now, there were feathers *everywhere*.

Piles of blond fluff all around the run. Inside the coop, I had to yard the feathers out by the bucketful. She was definitely setting another record—this time for the most epic hen molt ever.

All I could think was, who *is* this chicken? And what happened to Miss Broody?

After several days of marveling at all the feathers she was losing without going bald, I noticed her molting dialing down. The next time I entered the coop to clean it, there was a surprise.

Lying on the platform beneath the roost was a small brown egg!

IT WAS her first egg in *months*.

However, the fact that she'd laid her egg on the poo-catching platform meant Miss Broody must have forgotten something really important: what the nest boxes were for. So I moved the egg to one of the nests and left it. Two days later, I found a second egg. Right alongside her first one. So apparently the whole nest thing had come back to her.

And thus began Miss Broody's egg laying marathon.

First it was two eggs in four days, then three in a four-day period. Then seven eggs in eight days!

Her eggs started out on the small side—not quite as wee as a pullet egg, but a bit undersized. But they gradually became larger. We filled one empty egg carton, then started on a second. Miss Broody has never laid with this much regularity before—almost daily.

And come to think of it, not one of our Buff Orpington flock ever laid as consistently as this, not even in their first, vigorous months of laying. With all this champion egg production, I thought she deserved a new name. "Let's call her Missy," I said to John.

It was beyond rewarding to see our girl living a "henny" life again. And with the price of organic eggs *vrooming* in only one direction—up—it was especially gratifying to have homegrown eggs.

And I would enjoy every moment of Missy being a happy, productive hen.

56 * A HARD DECISION

This egg-laying spree of Missy's was impressive.

In September, she'd laid nineteen eggs in twenty-seven days! Yet given her history, if I was honest with myself, I figured it couldn't last.

I was right.

Around the first of October, the wildfire haze took a definite turn for the worse. The day the severe smoke rolled in, Missy didn't come out of the coop. Sure enough, when I went to check on her late in the afternoon, she was sunk onto the nest—hours after she would have been there to actually lay an egg.

Our girl, which we had so recently renamed "Missy," was once again Miss Broody.

The poor air quality might have had something to do with this new broody cycle—maybe she was laying low to escape the worst of the smoke, just like the other birds and bees and bunnies around our place had begun to do.

Still, broody was broody. I had a feeling, growing stronger by the day, that our little hen deserved better.

The fact that she was alone day after day, month after month —especially if she wasn't eating properly—would almost certainly make her simply pine away. The coming rain and cold would only make her solitary existence even more miserable.

Unless, despite all our precautions, a bobcat got her first.

During her laying spree, it seemed her state of high alert had faded a bit. But now that she was broody again, I guessed her anxiety had become entrenched in her muscle memory. Even when she was safe in her caged run, with me right there with her, she would cast nervous glances around constantly.

I had this sinking feeling—maybe an intuition—that eventually, the bobcat would kill her somehow. Either attack her outright...or scare her to death.

I just couldn't bear to have another hen killed. It wasn't only that I'd grown very fond of Miss Broody, especially after all she'd been through. More than ever, I was convinced that this scrappy little hen needed a much safer, and companion-filled place to live.

Yet where could I possibly find a good home for a hen that wasn't even laying?

The smoke-filled weeks slowly passed. Three weeks into October, when the first rain in two months fell, John and I rejoiced. Yet Miss Broody was an ongoing worry. And as November neared, I grew increasingly anxious about our little malnourished hen making it through the winter.

Remember our newfangled waterer and feeder that John purchased the previous year, just before the terrible winter storm? Their spectacularly short lives took on a new significance. In a vague kind of way, I wondered if our failed chicken improvements, even then, were trying to tell us something.

As the late October rain gathered strength, my worries for Miss Broody increased right along with it. The first of November brought a hard frost, cementing my sense that Miss Broody needed a new home. She was two-and-a-half years old;

she still had another two or three years of life at least. All I wanted for our little hen was to live out those days and years in warmth and safety.

That morning, as John's coffee maker burbled and I filled the kettle for my tea, I looked outside at the frozen ground and made a decision.

"Honey," I said to John, "I don't think we have a choice. We need to give Miss Broody away."

57 * MISS BROODY'S FATE HANGS IN THE BALANCE

*R*e-homing our hen was the right thing; John and I both knew it. Yet I had no idea where to start.

Since none of our neighbors were keeping hens anymore. I would have to venture further afield. I considered Craigslist to find a chicken owner who might take her on. Unfortunately, I'd heard the site had morphed into the Internet Wild West. My online privacy concerns spoke loudly: *do not go there.*

Okay, I was procrastinating. Yet Pollyanna that I am, I had the irrational hope that a better situation for Miss Broody would simply...come along. Appear like magic. Luckily, I still had a few weeks before any severe winter weather rolled in to figure it out.

But suddenly, I didn't.

THE FORECAST on the weather website made me blanch. A super-early northeaster was headed our way—and it wasn't just any northeaster gale. This one had temperatures dropping into the low teens.

This would be Miss Broody's first cold spell entirely on her own. A flock of hens, as I said before, generally huddles together on the roost at night. It's really cute, the way they line up on the roost, snugged up to each other as close as they can. That's how they keep each other warm.

But Miss Broody, alone in the coop, would have no other chicken to share body heat with.

I faced the hard fact that she could die from the cold. And if not in this northeaster, then the next one. And my inaction would be to blame.

Suddenly, my Pollyanna-ish "something will turn up" outlook evaporated. I needed to make a move right away.

BRIGHT AND EARLY ONE Monday morning, a new inspiration hit me: the Humane Society!

A couple of months before, I got reacquainted with a cousin who worked for the local branch. It turns out she loved the organization, and given my urgency, it seemed like an excellent bet. Maybe they would know some people who ran sort of an "old folks home" for chickens past their prime.

I checked their website—and what do you know, it was even better. They would take in farm animals. In fact, they would NOT turn away any animal.

Yet I hesitated. The organization seemed to have a very labyrinthine process to giving away your critter. Forms and checks and meetings. I was hoping for *simple*.

I considered a relatively new app that connects the people in your immediate neighborhood. Our nearest neighbor was on it, and the platform could hone in on a super local level. You can blame my privacy and tech-avoidance issues, and even more procrastination—yet I was reluctant to go this route too.

As the northeaster blew in, however, I was struck by one more idea. An option closer to home.

And I was determined to settle Miss Broody's fate while my resolution was strong.

58 * THE UNIVERSE POINTS THE WAY

I was acquainted with some neighbors about a mile up the county road.

One couple, Boomers like John and me, retired here about three years ago. I'm not too proud to admit that for me, their place inspired a *powerful* homestead envy. I called them the Gorgeous Homestead Family. They had 100 acres, the working part of their homestead tucked at the base of their own tree-covered foothill overlooking a broad, sunny pasture.

And that wasn't all. They had a gorgeous home with a wide, sunny deck along one entire side of the house. All summer long, they kept pots filled with flowers that cascaded over the railing.

What was just as enviable was the look-alike design of their brand-new monitor-style barn, sheds, and greenhouse, each covered with a green steel roof and rustic-looking cedar siding.

Even their very well organized chicken coop and pen matched the theme. For the perfect homesteady touch, near the driveway, they had a strategically placed antique tractor and cultivator.

This Boomer pair was really hardworking; everything on their place was immaculately maintained: vegetable garden perfectly tended, apples trees pruned, pasture and orchard mowed regularly, their little tree farm at the far end of the pasture was free of weeds, and the baby firs were thriving.

This couple was also very friendly. When they were working near the road or in their car passing me on my bike, we always waved to each other and said hello.

Still, the two of them seemed super busy, caring for a place so meticulously. I could see several hens in their chicken yard. But the birds were never out of their pen to free-range. Nor did the couple seem to hang out with their hens.

And their chicken coop was considerably farther from their house than ours was. If a predator menaced their chickens, who would know?

ANOTHER SET OF NEIGHBORS, around our age as well, lived just across from Gorgeous Homestead Family. I was also on a smile-and-wave basis with them, a "hi, how are you doing" kind of thing.

But I was a bit better acquainted with this twosome. Their small lot and house was right next to the road. After all, you can learn a lot about folks when you've cycled past their place, just a few feet away, at least a thousand times—my 16 years of near-daily bike rides since John and I moved to the Foothills.

If the couple, Joe and Janet, were working in their yard, I'd stop every now and then to inquire about their garden or pets, or any new project they were working on.

Their place, however, was entirely different from the Gorgeous Homestead. Due to health issues the last few years, Joe and Janet had been forced to neglect their vegetable garden, and fences were in a bit of disrepair. The yard was scattered with planting pots, fencing pieces, and various other garden equipment.

In all my interactions with them, however, I could tell they were good-hearted. And even more, *big* animal lovers, with several contented dogs hanging out on the front porch. I'd heard Janet had worked for the local veterinarian for a while, so the couple had occasionally fostered dogs.

That made sense—a new pup often showed up in the yard. A few of the dogs were canny escape artists too. Now and then, when one got loose, I'd commiserate with Joe and Janet, then keep an eye out for the fugitive.

Besides the dogs, they had lots of chickens, a mix of breeds scratching around the front yard. Their flock included a few Silkies—a rather exotic type in my mind, with their distinctive fluffy cap and leg feathers that looked like a feather boa.

What was different about Janet's chickens was that they were extraordinarily quiet. Nothing like ours had been, always clucking and *buck-buck-buck-gah!*-ing.

Janet kept a rooster, and even more amazingly, he was as quiet as the hens! John and I had never been tempted to get a rooster, even though, as I talked about before, there are many advantages to having one in your flock—most notably, to protect your hens from intruders.

But as I said, John and I had strong objections to a rooster's constant crowing. Even more, to their aggression. After we got our first flock, at a social gathering one evening, the conversation turned to chickens. An old friend told me all about a tough rooster in his childhood. This bird had not only gone after him, but jumped on his head! The story had really stuck with me.

So, yeah. No roosters for this girl.

SOME MONTHS BEFORE, long before I was looking for a new chicken home, I was biking past Joe and Janet's place, and she was tending her chickens in the front yard. Stopping for a quick hello, I couldn't help noticing something interesting. "Gosh," I said to her, "your rooster sure is mellow."

"Isn't he?" Janet smiled with pride. "I raised him from a newborn chick. He's very gentle. He doesn't really crow either."

That seemed extraordinary to me. I was the kind of hen-keeper who did the basics: I made sure our girls were fed and watered, and I would clean their coop and pen regularly. John and I would bring them fresh weeds to nibble on, and complimented them on their eggs.

Of course, I'd done the whole broody hen care too, schlepping them to the waterer and feeder. And sometimes feeling pretty cranky about it.

Janet was…different. She was not only a hen-lover…it was clear she was also a chicken-whisperer.

FROM THE ROAD, Janet and Joe's chicken "compound" looked pretty makeshift. Various fencing pieces were covered with a kind of tent structure composed of tarps and sheets of black plastic. To be honest, the whole affair looked a wee bit rickety. But the pen had to be warm; I could detect the glow of a heater even on only mildly chilly days.

And clearly, the compound was safe. Joe and Janet's was right next to their house—as in, just a few feet away. They would hear if anything was amiss. But what really showed their compound's safety was that Janet had a yard full of chickens, year in and year out. While John and I, despite our sturdy coop and run, had lost hens to predators right and left.

A total of fourteen hens in three different flocks.

FAST FORWARD TO my present dilemma with Miss Broody.

In our first, early November storm, she ended up making it through the worst days of the Northeaster. Luckily, she was still somewhat broody, so her body temperature was warmer than it normally would have been. I'd been pretty sure she'd get through it somehow—the December before, along with the other four hens, she'd survived the severe blizzard, with temperatures near zero, 15 degrees colder than this storm.

Still, I didn't want her to suffer through any more cold if I could help it. The third day of this frigid spell, the wind moderated a little. But it was still really chilly for gardening activities. And the days were short. By the time I got outside, the sun was already dipping in the west.

On cold days like this, I would debate my exercise: take a bikeride or walk? It would be a *cold* bikeride. Anytime the temperature was below freezing, despite my L.L. Bean polar mittens, I had a hard time keeping my fingers from turning into Popsicles. If I walked, I'd be far warmer all over, especially my hands.

But you see, I had this…*feeling*.

Not a niggling little idea in the back of my mind. This was a really strong conviction: everything in me pointed toward Janet's and Joe's direction. If I walked to their place, though, it would be a four mile trek up and back, about a mile longer than I was used to. Yet what was one little mile compared to Miss Broody's wellbeing?

But it would take forty minutes just to get there. And I wanted…no, I *needed* to be there sooner. Call it intuition, or the Universe. But something told me today was the day: I felt it was really important that I go up to Janet and Joe's house as soon as possible and see if they were home.

So feeling anxious, I clambered onto my bike and set off. While I long ago outgrew my extreme childhood shyness, I'm still quite an introvert. I wasn't sure I actually had the nerve to approach folks who were essentially strangers and ask them if they would be up for a hen that could be more trouble than she was worth.

Yet I had an even more powerful sense that it was now or never.

59 * SEND MORE CHICKENS

Cycling up the hill toward Janet and Joe's place, I was full of nervous energy. As I got closer to their house, I cautiously peered around. They were not only home, but outside!

The Universe was clearly, *really* telling me to go for it.

Joe was tooling around the garden on his riding lawn mower. I couldn't imagine much grass was growing in this freezing weather, but maybe he wanted to get a few licks on his lawn before nightfall. Janet was on the porch. I stopped at their gate to catch her eye, then waved to her.

She was probably a bit confused. I didn't normally get off my bike to chat when they were busy, but she made her way down the walkway to meet me.

To break the ice, I complimented her on their latest project. A large area around their veggie garden had been completely feral, a tangle of four-to-five foot high weeds gone to seed, plus wild blackberries, thimbleberries and an overgrown sunchoke patch. But suddenly this week, the space was magically cleared. "How did you do it?"

"Goats!" said Janet.

"No kidding," I said.

"We hired a few goats—it only took them three days. They'll eat anything."

"What a great idea." John and I had plenty of once-tamed-but-now-crazy wild spots in our yard that could have used the goat strategy. But I'd ask about goats another time.

Joe stopped the mower and moseyed over. From our previous brief conversations, I knew he was a fairly gregarious kind of guy and probably curious about my extended chat with his wife.

I said hello, then, "The reason I stopped is that I know you love animals."

Joe chuckled and Janet smiled a little.

Gathering my courage, I added quickly, "Do you have any ideas for a place to re-home a chicken?"

She didn't say a word, simply raised her hand, and waved it tentatively.

I burst into a grin. "You mean, you're interested?"

"I'd love to have her," said Janet.

I couldn't believe my luck. Or Miss Broody's. "She's broody," I said honestly, to give Janet a chance to back out. "Most of the time, in fact."

"I don't mind at all if she's broody," said Janet. "I just love chickens."

She stepped closer to me and touched my arm in a confiding way. "When our hens stop laying we don't get rid of them, they just stay with us for the rest of their lives."

"Yeah," said Joe, and chuckled again, "she won't let me invite them to Sunday dinner."

I laughed at his joke too. I told them a bit about our hen being the lone survivor of our flock—three picked off by a bobcat, and a fourth killed by a hawk.

"Years ago, a hawk got one of our hens," said Janet, "but with the dogs in the yard, the big cats don't really come around."

"That's a relief," I said. "I' afraid loneliness will finish off my little hen."

"Chickens really do need to be in a herd," Joe put in kindly. "They just don't do well alone. Bring her on over."

I was incredibly touched. Janet and Joe seemed perfect for Miss Broody, who might never lay again. "Sounds great," I said, my spirits rising. "Oh, something else—we just opened a new 25-pound sack of scratch I'd like to give you."

Janet looked pleased. "We'll be happy to have it."

"How about I'll come by in a couple of hours?"

"Anytime is fine," said Janet.

I suddenly noticed how the sun had dipped in the sky. "Are you sure? I don't want to disturb your dinner."

"Oh, we don't eat until eight or so," Janet said. "Even nine."

"So do we," I said, amazed that John and I weren't the only ones with a nutty evening schedule!

Joe grinned. "I don't even get going until around three in the afternoon."

Well, who knew that all this time there were kindred spirits just up the road! As I said goodbye, I felt even more positive about Miss Broody's future—that I'd not only found a home for her, but a *good* home.

And unlike with all our other two flocks, we wouldn't lose every last chicken to predators. My heart pinched, at the thought of letting go of hen-keeping. But at the same time, I felt some elation, at the chance to give our last girl a better life.

Instead of having Mother Nature take her from us.

When I got home from my bikeride, it was dusk. Miss Broody would probably be asleep.

Broody hens, once you get a good grip on them, will sort of go passive. Not go all flappy and cranky on you like active, wide awake chickens. But being moved at night? I could see even a broody hen could go into a panic.

Over the years, John and I had transported our three flocks of chickens in the middle of the day—and Holy Moly, did they get indignant, squawking and trying to escape as you stuck them inside a box.

Would disturbing a sleeping hen make her completely freak out? I would find out soon enough.

After changing into my warmest outdoor gear, I chopped some wood, then found a sizable, if tatty box to transport the hen. John was coming down with some kind of illness, so I wouldn't ask him to help with this whole enterprise. But he was game to bundle up and hold a lantern for me, for Miss Broody's relocation.

First, I put a couple of shovelfuls of wood chips into the box, so the hen would have a familiar smell around her. I sprinkled in a handful of scratch, in case a bit of food might have a calming effect. Once I brought the box to the coop area, it was go time.

From the other side of the chicken compound, John held the lantern high as I positioned the opened box just outside the people door. Moving quickly, I entered the coop and grasped the sleeping Miss Broody before she could react and bundled her out of the coop. She flapped her wings a bit feebly, but I was able to set her safely in the bottom of the box.

The box flaps were more flabby than I expected, but I secured them as best I could. With John lighting my way, I carried the box to the bed of his old Ford Ranger. Miss Broody had gone completely quiet, so hopefully I didn't have to worry about her trying to fly out of a moving pickup.

As John accompanied me to the truck, I noticed the stars

were out—a gorgeous night, but no moon to light my way. "Good luck, honey," he said.

"Thanks, I might need it." With a quick, "Bye," I clambered into the truck and started it up. To keep any jostling to a minimum, I tootled down our gravel lane in second gear, about 10 miles an hour, for the mile to the county road.

At the entrance to the main road, I put on the parking brake and hopped from the cab to check on the hen. She wasn't making a sound, so I peeked into the box and breathed a sigh of relief. Yep, she was still inside. Only one more mile to go.

On the main road, I kept my speed to about 15 mph, although the speed limit was 35 (and along this stretch, most people did 50). Envisioning some speedster rounding the curve and bashing into the Ranger from behind, I tried to turn on the hazard lights.

But they had apparently given up the ghost, like a lot of other functions in this 25 year-old pickup. With some trepidation, I crawled up the road, the whine of the engine the only sound.

Here on the county road, I felt a sense of the utter darkness: there were no streetlights, nor houses next to the road with yard lights. And with traffic very sparse this time of year, I met no other vehicles along the way.

Driving that mile seemed to take a very long time.

Approaching Janet and Joe's crowded driveway, my uncertainty returned. This whole project was so unlike me—approaching people I hardly knew, and asking them for a favor. I carefully pulled over into the small space available.

I picked my way around four or five vehicles, then Joe appeared seemingly out of nowhere. "Oh, hey! I'll get Janet."

"I'll get the hen," I said.

Before he could take three steps, the porchlights came on. Janet met me in their yard, as I trundled the unwieldly box in my arms. Following her on the narrow pathway, I barely avoided tripping on a hefty sack on the ground.

Black sunflower seeds! Janet's chickens were treated well.

Still, I wanted to give Joe and Janet an out. "Are you sure about this?" I asked Janet as we approached the chicken pen.

"Well, see my sign!" Just then, next to the pen gate, I saw a store-bought placard in a playful font: **Send More Chickens!**

60 * END OF AN ERA

*B*y the looks of her sign, Janet really *was* up for a non-laying, been-through-the-wars hen like Miss Broody!

As I stepped closer, toward the light shining in the chicken pen, I noticed the makeshift tent structure looked much sturdier than it had from the road. Catching the faint glow of an electric heater in the corner of my eye, I was struck by the impression of warmth and coziness. On this cold autumn night, the pen felt like a welcoming little island in the dark.

"A heater!" I said. Further evidence of Janet's hen devotion. "We never really tried to heat our coop."

"On cold mornings, I make warm oatmeal for them," said Janet with a touch of pride.

Wow. Just...*wow*. Miss Broody would get the royal treatment for sure.

Opening the gate to the compound, Janet said, "I have three chicken houses—where do you think we should put her?"

I could make out three small structures inside the tent—the closest one about four feet long and two and a half feet high and wide; the two others were smaller, not a whole lot bigger than the box I was carrying.

Giving me a choice was very lovely of Janet, I thought; she clearly didn't want to act like she was just taking over my hen. "Wherever you think is best." I was *so* not going to look this tremendous gift horse in the mouth!

"The big house, I think," said Janet.

With Miss Broody still asleep, I decided it would be less startling if only one human handled her. Cradling the box awkwardly in one arm, I opened the flaps with my free hand, and tilted the open end toward Janet. "Here she is."

Janet leaned in. "Oh, a blonde hen! I only have one." She reached for Miss Broody, much more confidently than I ever had.

I'd always picked up our hens by their bodies, my hands tight against their wings and midsection. So the way Janet went about lifting the hen surprised me.

She firmly grasped Miss Broody by the "drumstick" part of her legs.

As Miss Broody flapped her wings, Janet cradled her to her chest. "You're a sweetie," she crooned. The hen calmed almost instantly, and Janet quickly bundled her into the "Big House" coop.

It was done.

I was so touched that Janet already loved our little hen. But it was getting late. "Thank you so much," I said fervently, stepping away. Then I paused. "Goodbye, Missy," I called softly. I knew Miss Broody couldn't hear me but I needed to say it.

"You can come visit her," Janet said kindly.

"I just might do that." I thanked Janet and Joe one more time, and walked away from the circle of warmth and light to the Ranger, and started it up.

Making my way home, I felt bereft. But I reminded myself

that Miss Broody would have a wonderful life here. And a safe one.

Reaching home, I clambered out of the truck into the chilly night. I glanced up at the sky full of stars, sensing nature's benevolence. And gave thanks for good and generous people—and chicken-lovers—like Janet and Joe.

EPILOGUE

WISDOM HARD-EARNED

Four days later, I rode my bike past Miss Broody's new home and saw Janet and Joe's chickens in the front yard. Two blond hens that looked exactly alike scratched and pecked at the grass, one a little further away from the others.

It didn't matter to me which one was Miss Broody, it only mattered that my little hen had settled right in, and joined her new flock.

One month after that, I was away from our place again—this time to care for four family members ill with a severe flu. When I returned December 18th, that week before Christmas was a real doozie. While I was gone, a water line in our shop broke, and the night I came home we discovered a mouse infestation *inside* our house.

The next day, our area was hit by another Northeaster—with a foot of snow. With the high winds and extreme cold, it was the worst winter storm we'd experienced in our seventeen years in the Foothills.

If we'd still had Miss Broody, I really doubt she would have survived.

Trying to manage all these complications—catching up after ten days away, fixing the busted water pipe, cleaning up the mess, and dealing with mice frolicking around in both ends of the house—one thing seemed clear: John and I would never have had time to care for our little girl properly.

Miss Broody's new home had manifested just in the nick of time.

I'VE MISSED HAVING CHICKENS. But they're back in the neighborhood.

Gretchen and Alan, our hen benefactors, acquired a new flock of six—all blonde. Although one turned out to be a rooster, of course they remind me of our flock of Buffies, and seeing them makes me forlorn.

Still, it's lovely to see happy, active chickens now and then. And with our neighbors' recent security upgrades, including more heavy netting over a hurricane fence enclosure, their chickens should be safer than safe.

JOHN and I haven't talked much about getting more chickens. After what happened to our girls over the years, having hens wouldn't make sense unless we created an entirely new compound. We would need to dismantle the coop and pen and rebuild it right next to the house. *And* make the fencing tighter than Fort Knox.

The last three winters have taught us something else: the Foothills' winter storms are getting more extreme. The Northeaster low temperatures are getting lower; the most recent one was, for the first time, well below zero. To have chickens again, John and I would have to come up with a coop heating system as well.

The whole project would be a monumental undertaking.

And yet...

After the Universe so helpfully provided a new home for Miss Broody, it could be that *somehow*, if it's meant to be, a flock of hens will somehow come to us. And if it happens, *somehow* John and I will find the energy and money *and* inspiration to create an upgraded, heated compound.

But for now, I'm just going to see how life goes.

I still ride my bike past Janet and Joe's nearly every day. I can't help peering into the yard, trying to catch a glimpse of Miss Broody. I expect I always will.

And I know that if I do see her, I will once again feel the bittersweet sense that while giving up my sweet little hen was hard, it was the right thing to do.

I pass by our abandoned chicken compound every day too. Each time, I'm reminded of our girls Dottie and Chloe, Buffy and Little Britches, and all the others we lost. My memories flood in, the good and the bad.

Yet ensuring that Miss Broody was saved from a similar fate, I have a strong feeling that the short lives of our other girls weren't wasted. The hens brought joy and purpose to both John and me, and to every grandchild who interacted with them.

"LOVE IS A UNIVERSAL LANGUAGE, and anyone who loves chickens knows that they speak it too." —Melissa Caughey

Although our journey with our three flocks turned out to be often challenging, mostly a whole lot of work, and sometimes heartbreaking, I wouldn't have given it up for the world.

LITTLE FARM IN THE FOOTHILLS
—A SAMPLE

Little Farm in the Foothills:
A Boomer Couple's Search for the Slow Life
Little Farm in the Foothills Series, Book 1

*H*ere's a look at Susan's first homesteading memoir, *Little Farm in the Foothills: A Boomer Couple's Search for the Slow Life*. It's the story of moving from the city to create a small homestead in the woods—a warmhearted, true-life tale for gardeners, nature-lovers, and dreamers of all ages!

Chapter 1: Seeking Walden

It's said that if you want to figure out your life's passion, look at what you loved as a child. When I was growing up, I loved Barbies. You might think, there's a girl who'll go far, what with Astronaut Barbie and Internist Barbie and Professional Figure Skater Barbie. Actually, I predate all those ambitious, take-the-world-by-the-horns Barbies. In *my* time, back in the sixties, all Barbie did was sit around and look hot and wait for Ken to ask her out.

But I also loved to read, especially fairy tales like Sleeping Beauty, and stories about gutsy, courageous girls like Jo March and Laura Ingalls. And when I wasn't reading or hanging out with Barbie, Midge, and Skipper, I was playing in the woods behind our house. Maybe I was living out fantasies inspired by Sleeping Beauty's forest hideaway, or Laura's "Little House" series, but I found my bliss climbing trees, building forts and riding my bike around Woodland Hills, a new development perched on the rural edge of St. Cloud, Minnesota.

My husband, John, was an outdoorsy kid too, with a childhood a lot like mine. (Minus the Barbies.) Your mother sent you outside to play after breakfast, and except for lunch, you were supposed to stay there until it got dark or dinnertime, whichever came first. But then, you didn't really want to be indoors anyway. Certainly not John—from what I can tell, he *lived* "The Dangerous Book for Boys." He'd roam nearby woods and fields with his little gang of friends, playing Robin Hood or cowboys and Indians, coming home so dirty his mom would have to hose him down.

Later, as a young husband and father, John got his fresh air nurturing a small vegetable plot for his family. But it could be the outdoor activities so many of us love as adults, like camping, hiking, and gardening—and I hear vacations on working farms are getting popular!—are a way to free our inner tree-climbing, mud-lovin' child. To return to a simpler time, when most people lived on farms—or at least *knew* a farmer. A time when you spent far more of your life outside than in.

Whatever it is, I never stopped loving the outdoors, and John never lost his longing for wide open spaces...a love and longing we indulged with our mutual passion for gardening. But there came a time when we both yearned for a deeper connection with the land…for a more peaceful life, one more attuned to nature's pace. Okay, that sounds pretty highfalutin'—all we *thought* we wanted was more room for a kitchen garden, and a little quiet in which to enjoy it. Regardless of our goal, our journey to that life began the day we reached our tipping point with urban noise and traffic and crowds…when John and I bucked our play-it-safe, risk-averse natures and decided to leave the city. *Little Farm in the Foothills* is the tale of our fifty-something leap of faith, to seek out a slower, simpler, and more serene lifestyle on a rural acreage. And embrace a whole new way of living.

Who'd have guessed how complicated "simplicity" could get. Or that serenity and reinventing your life was no match made in heaven.

BEFORE I HIT my Boomer years, I'd never seriously considered living in the country.

Despite my woods-playing, I hadn't spent much time in the true boondocks. In elementary school, I'd been a Campfire Girl, but my group never went camping or sat around a campfire—much less lit one. I'd gone tent camping exactly once in my life, a post-high school girlfriend getaway memorable only for the fact that for the entire three days, we'd frozen our eighteen-year-old tushies off. In June!

Anyhow, I'm all for city comforts. Call me picky (I'm the first to admit I'm annoyingly germ-conscious), but I'd always been sort of revolted by the idea of an on-site septic system. There's all that "stuff" in a tank right next to your house, for Pete's sake. And I liked city water. The only well water I'd tasted was loaded with sulfurous compounds, and the rotten-egg smell wafting up from your glass would set off a gag reflex. I didn't want water from just *anywhere*—it could be unhygienic, okay? I have a B.S. in environmental studies. I *know* about contaminated groundwater. I wanted my drinking water from nice clean municipal water treatment plants.

But water was only a side issue. In my youth, I'd had the kind of country experience that would turn most people off permanently...

PRAISE FOR LITTLE FARM IN THE FOOTHILLS

"*S*ummer Reads—a Sense of Place," Award from the Washington State Library

"The Browne's foray into slower living…is an enjoyable read. Their delightful, yet very real, experiences in making the big leap toward their dreams make for a humorous and charming book." —Washington State Librarian Jan Walsh

"A delightful account." —*The Bellingham Herald*

LITTLE FARM in the Foothills and the sequel, **Little Farm Homegrown** are available for free at your local library; you can request the print or ebook version. You can also order a print copy at your neighborhood bookstore, or find the ebook at your favorite online retailer!

ACKNOWLEDGMENTS

I dedicate this book to our hen benefactors and neighbors extraordinaire Gretchen and Alan, who helped and supported us in every way through our chicken-raising adventures. Thank you dear friends, from the bottom of my heart.

I also dedicate **Little Farm in the Henhouse** to my mother Nanette, for encouraging my hen tales, particularly about Miss Broody, and for sharing her own chicken stories from her Illinois childhood.

I will never forget that John and I both owe a tremendous debt of gratitude to my mother and her husband Burl for providing "shelter from the storm" all those years ago. Without you, Mom and Burl, we would never have been able to have chickens…because Berryridge Farm would still be only a dream.

Besides my mom, boundless hugs go to our wonderful family—especially our children and grandchildren, for all the love, friendship and joy they bring into our lives.

I'm so thankful for my circle of creatives: Christine, Barbara, Deeann, Laine, Sarah and Sheryl. Your wonderful support and energy has been a guiding light for my writing…and creating!

Great appreciation to all the readers of my Little Farm books! Your kind comments and encouragement, and sharing the books with your friends and family, have inspired me to go the distance to Book 4.

I'm forever grateful to my husband John—not only for his wonderful photography that adorns the covers of my Little Farm books, but for all our hen wrangling together. His ideas and artistic eye, and especially his support and encouragement means everything to me. I feel eternally blessed to have him as my true-blue partner all our years together.

About the Author

Susan Colleen Browne is a graduate of the College of the Environment , Western Washington University. She's the author of an award-winning memoir, *Little Farm in the Foothills*, the sequel, *Little Farm Homegrown*, and a food gardening guide, *Little Farm in the Garden*.

Susan weaves her love of Ireland and her passion for country living into her Village of Ballydara series, novels and stories of love, friendship and family set in the Irish countryside. Her latest Irish novels are **Becoming Emma** and **The Fairy Cottage of Ballydara**, with more books on the way!

She has also created a fantasy-adventure series for tweens set in the Pacific Northwest. A community college instructor, Susan runs a little homestead with her husband John in the Pacific Northwest, USA.

When Susan isn't wrangling chickens or tending vegetable beds, she's working on her next Village of Ballydara book!

Find her at www.susancolleenbrowne.com and www.susancolleenbrowne.substack.com

BOOKS BY SUSAN COLLEEN BROWNE

The Village of Ballydara Series
It Only Takes Once, Book 1 (print and ebook)
Mother Love, Book 2 (print and ebook)
The Hopeful Romantic, Book 3 (print and ebook)
The Galway Girls, Book 4 (print and ebook)
The Secret Well, short story ebook
A Christmas Visitor, short story ebook and the sequel to *The Secret Well*
The Little Irish Gift Shop, Book 5
Becoming Emma, Book 6
Becoming Emma, Special Edition
The Fairy Cottage of Ballydara, Book 7

Little Farm in the Foothills Series
Little Farm in the Foothills: A Boomer Couple's Search for the Slow Life, Book 1 (print, ebook and digital audiobook)
Little Farm Homegrown: A Memoir of Food-Growing, Midlife, and Self-Reliance on a Small Homestead, Book 2 (print, ebook and digital audiobook)
Little Farm in the Garden: A Practical Mini-Guide to Raising Selected Fruits and Vegetables Homestead-Style, Book 3 (print, ebook and digital audiobook)
Little Farm in the Henhouse: A True-Life Tale of Hen-Keeping, Homestead-Style, Book 4, (print and ebook)

The Morgan Carey Series for Tweens, set in the Pacific Northwest
Morgan Carey and The Curse of the Corpse Bride, Book 1, a lighthearted Halloween story (print, ebook and digital audiobook)

Morgan Carey and The Mystery of the Christmas Fairies, Book 2, a gentle fantasy (print and ebook), set in the Foothills!

The Secret Astoria Scavenger Hunt, Book 3, a haunted house adventure (print and ebook)

Susan's books are available for **free** in ebook and print format at your local library—all you have to do is put in a request, or use the Libby library app.

You can also order them from your neighborhood bookstore or find them at your favorite online retailer!

FOOD GARDENING, HEN-KEEPING AND BACKYARD FARMING RESOURCES

Carpenter, Novella. *Farm City: The Education of an Urban Farmer.* Penguin Books, 2010.

Deppe, Carol. *The Resilient Gardener: Food production and Self-Reliance in Uncertain Times.* White River Junction, Vt.: Chelsea Green, 2010.

Kimball, Kirsten. *The Dirty Life: A Memoir of Farming, Food and Love.* New York: Scribner, 2011.

Kingsolver, Barbara, et al. *Animal, Vegetable, Miracle: A Year of Food Life.* New York: HarperCollins, 2007.

Solomon, Steve. *Gardening When it Counts: Growing Food in Hard Times.* Gabriola Island, B.C., Canada: New Society Publishers, 2006.

Mother Earth News Magazine, www.motherearthnews.com

Joel Salatin, owner of Polyface Farms in Virginia and the author of many books including *You Can Farm* and *Folks, This Ain't Normal*; Mr. Salatin also appears in documentary, "Food, Inc." www.polyfacefarms.com

"The Biggest Little Farm" documentary film, 2018, www.biggestlittlefarmmovie.com

To connect to farmers, gardeners, homesteaders, and other

food-growers in your area, you can check your state's university agriculture extension programs, your local food co-op, and local farmer's markets.

Last but not least...

If you're interested in the way hens' brains work, I heartily recommend *How to Speak Chicken* by Melissa Caughey—a true chicken-whisperer. This charming read includes lots of fascinating information about chickens generally, along with stories about her own "girls." There's plenty of intel about roosters too.

Throughout her book, Ms. Caughey illustrates that hens are *far* more intelligent than humans give them credit for...and far wiser than most folks have ever suspected.

www.ingramcontent.com/pod-product-compliance
Lightning Source LLC
Chambersburg PA
CBHW032104090426
42743CB00007B/224